Group's Serengeti Trek
Where Kids are Wild about God

LION CUB CLUB

PRESCHOOL DIRECTOR MANUAL

Group

Loveland, Colorado
www.groupvbs.com

Group resources actually work!

This Group resource helps you focus on **"The 1 Thing™"**—a life-changing relationship with Jesus Christ. "The 1 Thing" incorporates our **R.E.A.L.** approach to ministry. It reinforces a growing friendship with Jesus, encourages long-term learning, and results in life transformation, because it's:

Relational
Learner-to-learner interaction enhances learning and builds Christian friendships.

Experiential
What learners experience through discussion and action sticks with them up to 9 times longer than what they simply hear or read.

Applicable
The aim of Christian education is to equip learners to be both hearers and doers of God's Word.

Learner-based
Learners understand and retain more when the learning process takes into consideration how they learn best.

Lion Cub Club Preschool Director Manual
Copyright © 2005 Group Publishing, Inc.

All rights reserved. No part of this book may be reproduced in any manner whatsoever without prior written permission from the publisher, except where noted on handouts and in the case of brief quotations embodied in critical articles and reviews. For information, write Permissions, Group Publishing, Inc., Dept. PD, P.O. Box 481, Loveland, CO 80539.

Visit our Web sites:
www.group.com
www.groupvbs.com
www.groupoutlet.com

Thanks to our talented VBS curriculum team!
Gwyn D. Borcherding, Jessica Broderick, Jody Brolsma, Teryl Cartwright, Shelly Dillon, Enelle G. Eder, Josh Emrich, Lynne Foster, Cindy S. Hansen, Lisa Harris, Tracy K. Hindman, Alison Imbriaco, Mikal Keefer, Julie Lavender, Maura Link, Linda Marcinkowski, Katie Martinez, Pat Miller, Kari K. Monson, Barbie Murphy, Peggy Naylor, Jane Parenteau, Janis Sampson, Joani Schultz, Larry Shallenberger, Pamela Shoup, Rodney Stewart, Bonnie Temple

Illustrator: Corbin Hillam

Unless otherwise indicated, all Scripture quotations are taken from the *Holy Bible*, New Living Translation, copyright © 1996. Used by permission of Tyndale House Publishers, Inc., Wheaton, Illinois 60189. All rights reserved. (Day 4 Treasure Verse from the New Century Version.)

ISBN 0-7644-2790-3
Printed in the United States of America.
10 9 8 7 6 5 4 3 2 1   07 06 05

CONTENTS

LION CUB CLUB
PRESCHOOL DIRECTOR MANUAL

Welcome to Serengeti Trek! 5

Your Role at Serengeti Trek 7

Serengeti Trek Overview 12

Before the Trek Begins 14

Lion Cub Club Basic Supplies 17

Serengeti Trek Safety Tips 19

What's a Cub Crew? 20

What's Operation Kid-to-Kid™? 22

What's the Daily Challenge™? 26

Serengeti Trek Is
Crawling With New Friends! 27

DAY 1 (Know God.) 29

DAY 2 (Talk to God.) 49

DAY 3 (Tell about God.) 65

DAY 4 (Love God.) 81

DAY 5 (Work for God.) 97

LION CUB CLUB PRESCHOOL DIRECTOR MANUAL

WELCOME TO SERENGETI TREK!

A giraffe casually nibbles leaves from a lush acacia tree.

A lion crouches in the tall grass, watching a herd of zebras.

Suddenly an elephant thunders by in a cloud of dust.

And you? You're standing on the vast savanna, gearing up for the adventure of a lifetime on a Serengeti Trek—where kids are wild about God!

Serengeti Trek is teeming with fun for kids, teenagers, and adults. Everyone involved in *this* VBS will pounce into God's Word…and will never be the same again! As kids explore amazing Bible adventures, they'll take part in Daily Challenges that encourage them to apply Bible truths to everyday life.

If you haven't used Group's VBS materials before, you're in for a real treat. Serengeti Trek is an exciting, fun-filled, Bible-based program your kids will love. (We know because we tested everything in a field test last summer. Look for the "Hints From the Herd" to learn how our discoveries will make *your* program the best!)

Preschoolers begin each day's adventures with the older kids at Sing & Play Roar, where they'll sing and do fun motions to high-energy Bible songs that introduce kids to the concepts they'll be learning that day. Then preschoolers join their Cub Crews to participate in age-appropriate, hands-on learning activities at Lion Cub Club. Your little adventurers will also get to have scrumptious snacks from Watering Hole Snacks, view the Chadder's Serengeti Trek Adventure video, and join the older children for the closing at The Mane Event.

TREK TIPS

"Our preschoolers will want to be like the big kids! Let's let them go to the Serengeti Stations too." Think again! Although your little ones do want to emulate the big kids, the activities in the elementary Serengeti Station leader manuals haven't been designed for preschoolers. By using the activities in this director manual, you can be sure that every activity is age-appropriate and designed specifically for children ages three to five years old.

TREK TIPS

Cub Crew Leaders will provide plenty of extra supervision for wiggly preschoolers. But it's always a good idea to have an extra pair of hands to help keep everything under control. To make your job even easier, we recommend having a team of leaders. Leaders can alternate the days for which they prepare, or they can share leadership for portions of each day. For children ages three to five, plan to have one Lion Cub Club Director for every forty-five students, then build your staff from there.

INTRODUCTION

LEADING LION CUB CLUB IS EASY AND FUN!

You'll enjoy your role and be most successful as a Lion Cub Club Director if you…

- 🐾 enjoy working with small children;
- 🐾 stock your room with blocks, dress-up clothes, modeling dough, and other age-appropriate toys and materials;
- 🐾 crouch down and interact with children at their eye level;
- 🐾 have a go-with-the-flow attitude;
- 🐾 use simple language that preschoolers can understand; and
- 🐾 model God's love in everything you say and do.

YOUR ROLE AT SERENGETI TREK

Here's what's expected of you before, during, and after Serengeti Trek.

BEFORE SERENGETI TREK

- Attend scheduled Serengeti Trek training.
- Pray for the kids who will attend your church's Serengeti Trek.
- Plan your wardrobe. Ask your Serengeti Trek Director (otherwise known as your church's VBS director) what you should wear each day. Adult staff T-shirts (available from Group Publishing and your local Christian bookstore) help kids identify you and help you identify other leaders. You might consider wearing khaki shorts, a tan vest, and hiking boots.
- Read this Lion Cub Club Preschool Director Manual. Each day's programming contains a variety of activities for you to choose from. You can set up all the activities or just a few. Use the ones that work best for your kids.
- With the help of your Serengeti Trek Director, recruit Cub Crew Leaders for your preschoolers. A Cub Crew Leader can be anyone from a high school student to a senior citizen. Crew leaders just need to love the Lord and love children. Although Cub Crew Leaders don't have to prepare anything, their presence, love, and guidance form the backbone of your program. You'll want to recruit one Cub Crew Leader for every three to five preschoolers. And middle school students make great helpers—for you! Ask middle schoolers to set up Cub Club Craft Play or Preschool Playtime activities, or have them help with Bible dramas.
- If Cub Crew Leaders can't come to leader training, distribute photocopies of the "For Preschool Cub Crew Leaders Only" handouts from the Director Manual (pp. 143-144). The handouts contain information to help Cub Crew Leaders succeed. You'll want to meet briefly with your Cub Crew Leaders to go over this information, answer questions, and let them know about their special responsibilities as preschool helpers.

To *really* prepare your Cub Crew Leaders, we've provided you with another handy resource. The Preschool Crew Leader Pocket Guide is a 16-page booklet filled with helpful tips, an overview chart, and guidelines that will make your Cub Crew Leaders the best ever! Preschool Crew Leader Pocket Guides are available from Group Publishing and your local Christian bookstore.

- Check with your Serengeti Trek Director to see about providing special hats for your Cub Crew Leaders. Then make sure to point out the hats to the preschoolers. The hats will make it easier for children to identify the Cub Crew Leaders.

HINTS FROM THE HERD

During our field test, we tried all the options we've given you in this manual. As a result, our leaders felt a little rushed to get through everything. (We'll be honest; they were worn out!) We've given you plenty of activities to choose from, but you don't need to do all of them. Choose the ones that work best for the number of preschoolers you'll have, your facility, and your staff.

HINTS FROM THE HERD

We found our middle school-age Assistant Cub Crew Leaders and our high school-age Cub Crew Leaders to be very helpful and loving. They interacted well with the preschoolers. However, we discovered that some lacked initiative because they didn't always know what to do next. When we explained their specific tasks to them ahead of time or wrote things on paper, they were empowered and more focused on their roles.

Cub Crew Leader caps will help little ones *spot* their leaders at Serengeti Trek!

INTRODUCTION

TREK TIPS

If the Cub Crew Leaders can't come to the training, we highly recommend that you distribute copies of the Go Wild! Recruiting, Overview, and Pass-Along Training DVD. This "pass-along" training video is filled with practical, helpful tips for Cub Crew Leaders. Cub Crew Leaders are an integral part of children's Bible-learning experiences at Serengeti Trek, so provide these leaders with any and every training opportunity you can.

TREK TIPS

Here's a list of some Serengeti creatures to help you make creative Cub Crew signs: monkeys, baboons, lions, leopards, wildebeests, frogs, snakes, water buffaloes, cheetahs, crowned cranes, giraffes, elephants, zebras, hippos, rhinos, and lizards.

TREK TIPS

Although it may be tempting to include everyone in the VBS fun, we encourage you to use this program only with children who are at least three years old. Use the Serengeti Babies: Infants, Toddlers, and Twos Director Manual to create a special program for your youngest adventurers! (The Serengeti Babies: Infants, Toddlers, and Twos Director Manual is available from Group Publishing or your local Christian bookstore.)

- To better prepare your Cub Crew Leaders, you might want to get together with them just before each day's session begins. Meet for five minutes to allow the Cub Crew Leaders to hear what the Bible story will be, find out how Cub Club Craft Play works, and receive any important updates. And be sure to pray! You'll find it's a valuable time for everyone.

- Preview the *Chadder's Serengeti Trek Adventure* video. By viewing the video before Serengeti Trek, you'll know what to expect and can tell the children what to expect each day. Children will pay closer attention and retain more if they know what to watch for.

  (*Chadder's Serengeti Trek Adventure* is now available on DVD! If your church has DVD capabilities—or you're willing to bring your DVD player from home—this is the easy, no-hassle way to go.)

- Ask the Sing & Play Roar Leader and the Mane Event Leader to reserve places up front for the preschoolers each day. Label the seating areas with Lion Cub Club signs or flags. The preschoolers won't be able to read the signs, but the older kids will.

- Use the clip art of the baby Bible Memory Buddies® (from the *Serengeti Trek Clip Art, Song Lyrics, and Decorating* CD) to make large signs for each Cub Crew. To keep things simple, make each sign a different color. Then name each crew after that color—you might have the Yellow Giraffes or the Blue Elephants. This makes it easy for the little ones to find their crews each day.

- Gather the supplies you'll need for the activities you've chosen. It may be helpful to meet with the Serengeti Trek Director to go over the supply lists. Let the director know what supplies you have or can collect on your own and what supplies you'll need to collect from church members or purchase. Open communication will make your job easier!

- Designate a special area where the preschoolers will be picked up each day. Tell the Mane Event Leader where you plan to have the children gather at the end of the day.

- Prepare parents for what to expect. Some parents may be skeptical about having their children in a combined-age class. ("My five-year-old won't want to play with three-year-olds!" "My three-year-old will get trampled by all those five-year-olds!") Reassure parents that all activities are designed (and tested) to build relationships, encourage teamwork, and highlight children's abilities. Make photocopies of the letter on page 21, and give the letter to parents as they register their preschoolers for Serengeti Trek.

- Be sure to look over the registration forms to make yourself aware of any food allergies the children may have. If any children do have allergies, meet with the Watering Hole Snacks Leader to arrange for a suitable alternative.

Mixed-age Cub Crews are great for the whole herd!

DURING SERENGETI TREK

- Welcome the children individually as they arrive. Let them know you're glad they've come to Serengeti Trek. Keep in mind that some of the younger preschoolers may feel anxious about leaving their parents or caregivers, so your smiling, welcoming presence is important!

- Meet and greet parents or caregivers, and encourage them to explore your room with their preschoolers. Explain that after Day 1, they will drop off their children in the Sing & Play Roar area and pick up their little ones in another designated area. Reassure parents and caregivers that the Cub Crew Leaders will stay with the children until all the children have been picked up.

- Assure parents that their children will have a blast in Lion Cub Club. Some parents may want their preschoolers to join elementary Safari Crews (with older siblings). Firmly insist that the activities at Lion Cub Club are the *best* ones for preschoolers. It's really unfair to elementary kids, crew leaders, and even preschoolers to move children into activities that aren't age appropriate.

- *On Day 1 only*, have the preschoolers report directly to Lion Cub Club after registration instead of going to Sing & Play Roar. This will help the children settle into their new surroundings before they prepare the snacks for that day's Serengeti Trek. Make sure the Cub Crew Leaders have set up undirected activities, such as blocks, dress-up, or modeling-dough stations, for children who arrive early.

- On Days 2 through 5, have the preschoolers report directly to Sing & Play Roar. Have Cub Crew Leaders meet the children at the door. When all the kids in their Cub Crews have arrived, the Cub Crew Leaders can lead children to the seating area that has been reserved for them.

- On Day 1, help the preschoolers prepare snacks for all the children at Serengeti Trek. This may sound impossible, but it's not! The Watering Hole Snacks Leader will help you. Consult with him or her to determine whether to do this project in Lion Cub Club or in the Watering Hole Snacks area.

  Children will learn important sharing and cooperation skills as they work together to make the snacks. Smiles will appear on every face when the preschoolers realize their accomplishment. It really works!

- To help create a fun atmosphere and reinforce Bible learning, play the *Sing & Play Roar Music* audiocassette or CD as the children enter and leave Lion Cub Club. (Preschoolers will be singing these songs during Sing & Play Roar and will *love* them!)

- Use the Safari Sing-Along songs (at the end of each day's lesson) as transition songs, traveling songs, or time-fillers. Photocopy the songs, and keep them handy each day. You'll find that preschoolers love these easy-to-sing tunes—and they reinforce the daily Bible Point!

- Tell the daily Bible story with expression and enthusiasm. (Be familiar with your "script" so you don't have to read the story straight from this leader manual.) Engage children with eye contact and drama.

- Help the Cub Crew Leaders as they interact with the preschoolers, and reinforce the connection of the day's activities to the Bible Point. Encourage the Cub Crew Leaders to work closely with the children so you have the freedom to travel among the Cub Crews.

INTRODUCTION

TREK TIPS

If you have more than 25 preschoolers, you'll find it less chaotic to bring the children back to the Lion Cub Club room after The Mane Event. Ask the parents to remain outside the room until the Cub Crew Leaders make sure that the children have all their crafts and other items from the day's activities. Then let parents come in to pick up their kids.

TREK TIPS

To help latecomers find you on Days 2 through 5, put a sign on the door of the Lion Cub Club room to direct parents to bring their children to the Sing & Play Roar area.

HINTS FROM THE HERD

We had several Cub Crew Leaders get sick during the week, so we had to bring in new crew leaders. The inconsistency was hard on the preschoolers, who really need one reliable leader. Kids who had the same leader all week felt more comfortable and confident at Serengeti Trek and got more out of their Cub Crew relationships. Help crew leaders understand the importance of their role so they can commit to an entire week of fun at Serengeti Trek.

INTRODUCTION

TREK TIPS

What's in a name? Everything…at least for preschoolers! Encourage your Cub Crew Leaders to learn their Cub Crew members' names and to use the children's names every day. (And have the Cub Crew Leaders tell the preschoolers their names!) Not only is this simple connection affirming, but it also builds meaningful relationships. What better way to model God's love!

TREK TIPS

If you have more than one hundred (elementary and preschool) children at your VBS, you may want preschoolers to put their crafts and Cub Club Bible Books in a special area of your room. Make copies of the Cub Crew signs, and post the signs along one wall of Lion Cub Club. After The Mane Event, preschoolers can return to your room and wait to be picked up near the signs.

- Repeat the daily Bible Point often. It's important to say the Point just as it's written. Repeating the Bible Point again and again will help the children remember it so they can apply it to their lives. Whenever the children hear the Bible Point, they'll respond by saying "Wow!" in a stage whisper—almost like a roar. Children will also make a sign for "Wow!" by bringing their fists near their chin, then flinging their fingers out when they say "Wow!" Each Lion Cub Club activity suggests ways to include the Bible Point.

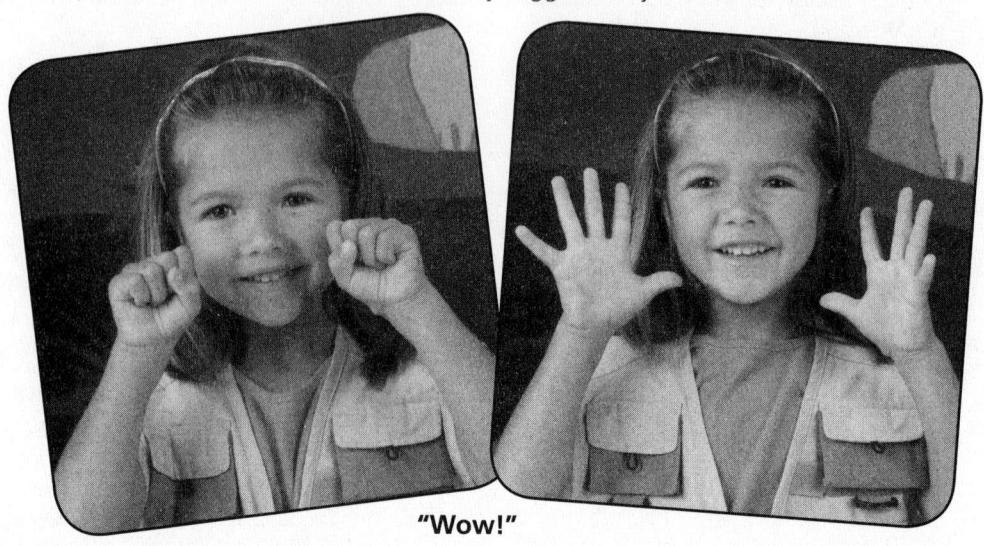

"Wow!"

- Set up a variety of Cub Club Craft Play and Preschool Playtime activities each day.

DAILY CHALLENGE™

- Remind children of their Daily Challenges. The Daily Challenge™ is an exciting way to help children apply Bible truths to real life…right away! During Lion Cub Club, point out when a child or crew leader has shown God's love to you. Talk about how exciting it is to see God's love grow in preschoolers' lives! (You can learn more about the Daily Challenge on page 26 of this manual.)

- Accompany children when they leave Lion Cub Club to go outside or to join in other activities. Remind the children to hold hands, or have children hold on to ropes to keep everyone together. (You might call the ropes "lion tails"!)

- Be sure to incorporate some time for free play into your daily schedule. Most VBS programs last two to three hours, which is a long time for preschoolers to engage in structured programming.

- Consider having the Cub Crew Leaders collect the children's crafts and bring them to The Mane Event at the end of the day. If the preschoolers have their crafts with them, parents and caregivers won't have to make an extra trip to your classroom.

> **Preschoolers may not be used to leaving the nest. Encourage your crew leaders to help little ones feel safe, welcome, and loved at Lion Cub Club.**

AFTER SERENGETI TREK

- Return equipment to its proper place.
- Use the following ideas to remind children of God's love all year long:
  - Phone neighborhood kids who participated in your Serengeti Trek program, and invite them to Sunday school.
  - Send Serengeti Trek follow-up postcards.
  - Use the Safari Sing-Along tunes and repeat Cub Club Craft Play or Preschool Playtime activities in Sunday school or midweek classes.
  - Show the *Chadder's Serengeti Trek Adventure* video in your Sunday school or midweek classes.
  - Purchase a Chadder Chipmunk™ puppet to use in your preschool classes.

Preschoolers will love watching Chadder Chipmunk! In fact, preschool children in previous Group VBS programs repeatedly asked, "When is Chadder coming to our room?" If you want to add extra fun to Lion Cub Club, purchase a Chadder Chipmunk puppet (available at www.groupoutlet.com). Use the following ideas to incorporate Chadder Chipmunk into your daily activities:

- Have Chadder welcome preschoolers as they arrive.
- Have Chadder take part in Safari Sing-Along with the children.
- Have Chadder search for a Bible Memory Buddy® each day.
- Have Chadder participate in games.
- Have Chadder introduce the Bible story.
- Have Chadder ask questions about the Bible Point or the Bible story.
- Have Chadder introduce his video presentation.

SERENGETI TREK OVERVIEW

This is what everyone else is doing! During Serengeti Trek, the daily Bible Point is carefully integrated into each activity to reinforce Bible learning. Lion Cub Club activities will fill most of your time.

	Bible Point	Bible Story	Treasure Verse	Sing & Play Roar	Bible Expedition	Wild Games
DAY 1	Know God.	Gideon defeats the Midianites (Judges 7:1-22).	"I know the greatness of the Lord" (Psalm 135:5).	• Hear the Bible story of Gideon defeating the Midianites. • Meet Zach the Zebra Bible Memory Buddy. • Choose Safari Crew jobs. • Learn: "He's the King" "My Jesus, He Loves Me" "I Want to Know You (In the Secret)" "To God Be the Glory"	• Become part of Gideon's army. • Light a torch and know that God will help Gideon. • Tell about someone they know and trust.	Play: • That Face Rings a Bell • Gideon's Army Tag • "Rocka" My Soul
DAY 2	Talk to God.	Daniel prays and is sent to the den of lions (Daniel 6:1-28).	"Pray at all times" (Ephesians 6:18).	• Hear the Bible story about Daniel praying and being sent to the den of lions. • Meet Roary the Lion Bible Memory Buddy. • Learn: "Lovely Noise" "Must Be Done in Love" "Let Us Pray"	• Listen to the lions roar as they hear the story of Daniel. • Discover that Daniel prayed no matter what and that we can talk to God too. • Use a Prayer Pal to talk to God.	Play: • Getting Connected • Daniel in the Den • Stretch Yourself
DAY 3	Tell about God.	Shadrach, Meshach, and Abednego stand up for God (Daniel 3:1-30).	"I will tell of all the marvelous things you have done" (Psalm 9:1b).	• Hear the Bible story about Shadrach, Meshach, and Abednego standing up for God. • Meet Elaine the Crane Bible Memory Buddy. • Learn: "Famous One" "Use Me"	• Experience the Bible story of the three friends. • See a hot experiment, and decide if they would stand up for God. • Tell about modern-day idols.	Play: • Seen but Not "Herd" • Trek Traveling • Marvelous Madhouse
DAY 4	Love God.	Jesus dies and rises again (John 19:1–20:18).	"We love because God first loved us" (1 John 4:19).	• Hear the Bible story about Jesus dying and rising again. • Meet Gigi the Giraffe Bible Memory Buddy. • Learn: "More Love, More Power"	• Visit the garden and investigate the empty tomb. • Hear Jesus call Mary's name. • Find "evidence" to prove Jesus' resurrection.	Play: • Wet Sponge Juggle • Catch Me! • Wild About What?
DAY 5	Work for God.	Paul and Silas worship God in prison (Acts 16:16-40).	Work hard and cheerfully as though for the Lord (adapted from Colossians 3:23).	• Hear the Bible story about Paul and Silas worshipping God in prison. • Meet Lug the Elephant Bible Memory Buddy. • Review Sing & Play Roar songs.	• Become prisoners in a Bible-times jail. • Sing and praise God in jail.	Play: • Sweet 'n' Sour Smiles • Serengeti Saucers • Work-for-God Tag

This overview shows you what the older kids will be doing. Your preschoolers will participate in the shaded activities. Be sure to check with your Serengeti Trek Director to see when your little adventurers will join the fun!

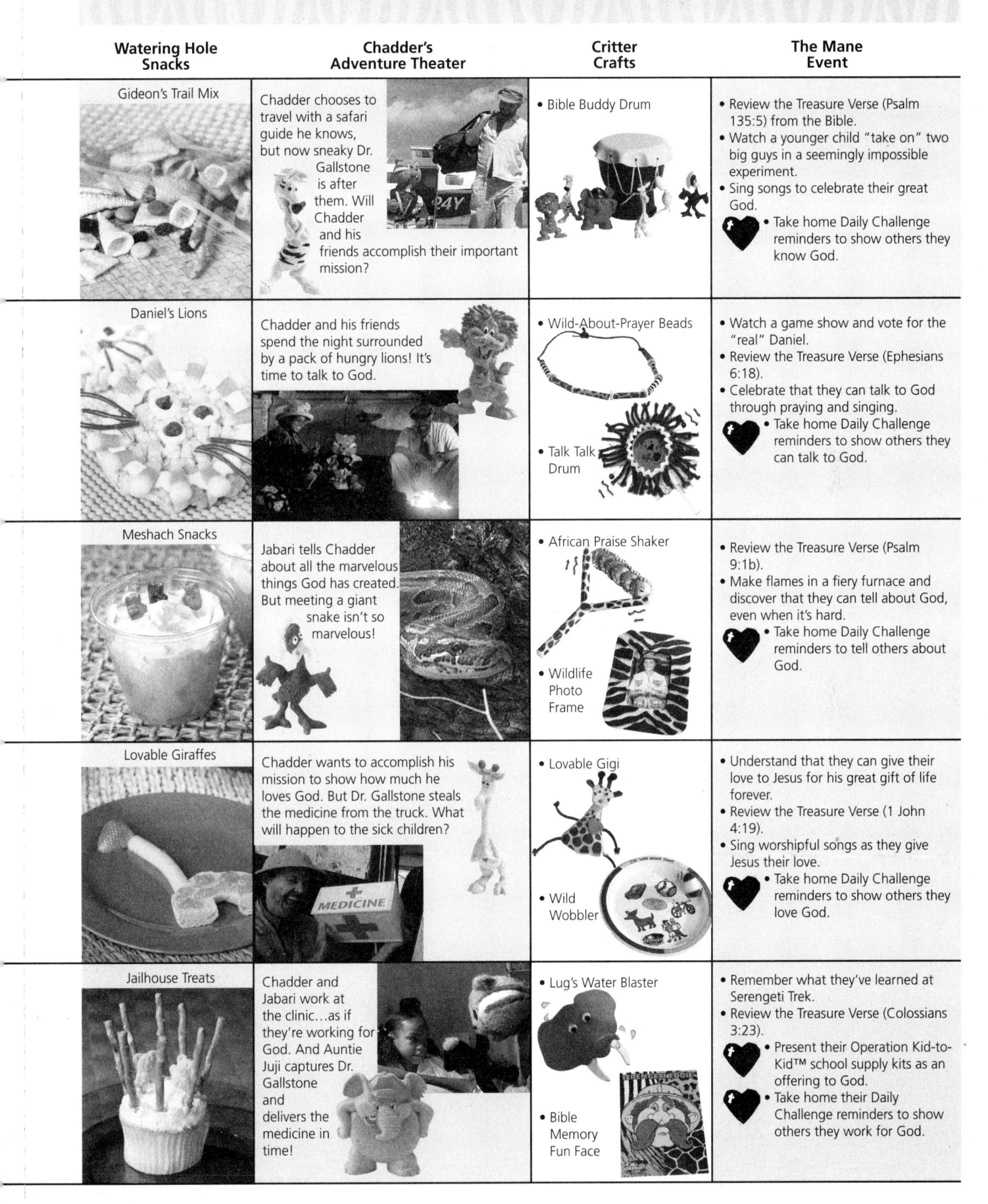

Watering Hole Snacks	Chadder's Adventure Theater	Critter Crafts	The Mane Event
Gideon's Trail Mix	Chadder chooses to travel with a safari guide he knows, but now sneaky Dr. Gallstone is after them. Will Chadder and his friends accomplish their important mission?	• Bible Buddy Drum	• Review the Treasure Verse (Psalm 135:5) from the Bible. • Watch a younger child "take on" two big guys in a seemingly impossible experiment. • Sing songs to celebrate their great God. ♥ • Take home Daily Challenge reminders to show others they know God.
Daniel's Lions	Chadder and his friends spend the night surrounded by a pack of hungry lions! It's time to talk to God.	• Wild-About-Prayer Beads • Talk Talk Drum	• Watch a game show and vote for the "real" Daniel. • Review the Treasure Verse (Ephesians 6:18). • Celebrate that they can talk to God through praying and singing. ♥ • Take home Daily Challenge reminders to show others they can talk to God.
Meshach Snacks	Jabari tells Chadder about all the marvelous things God has created. But meeting a giant snake isn't so marvelous!	• African Praise Shaker • Wildlife Photo Frame	• Review the Treasure Verse (Psalm 9:1b). • Make flames in a fiery furnace and discover that they can tell about God, even when it's hard. ♥ • Take home Daily Challenge reminders to tell others about God.
Lovable Giraffes	Chadder wants to accomplish his mission to show how much he loves God. But Dr. Gallstone steals the medicine from the truck. What will happen to the sick children?	• Lovable Gigi • Wild Wobbler	• Understand that they can give their love to Jesus for his great gift of life forever. • Review the Treasure Verse (1 John 4:19). • Sing worshipful songs as they give Jesus their love. ♥ • Take home Daily Challenge reminders to show others they love God.
Jailhouse Treats	Chadder and Jabari work at the clinic…as if they're working for God. And Auntie Juji captures Dr. Gallstone and delivers the medicine in time!	• Lug's Water Blaster • Bible Memory Fun Face	• Remember what they've learned at Serengeti Trek. • Review the Treasure Verse (Colossians 3:23). ♥ • Present their Operation Kid-to-Kid™ school supply kits as an offering to God. ♥ • Take home their Daily Challenge reminders to show others they work for God.

BEFORE THE TREK BEGINS

LION CUB CLUB PREPARATION

TREK TIPS

If you have more than twenty-five preschool children and don't have access to a large room, we suggest setting up two or more small rooms and running two separate Lion Cub Club programs on alternating schedules. That way you only have to set up once, and children can move between the rooms. Or you can have Cub Crews form two groups; while half of the Cub Crews are at Cub Club Craft Play, the other crews can be at Preschool Playtime.

- Work with your Serengeti Trek Director to choose a room for Lion Cub Club. You'll want a fairly large room that you can leave set up all week. If your church has a preschool or kindergarten Sunday school room, you might want to use it. The illustration below shows one way you might want to set up your Lion Cub Club area.

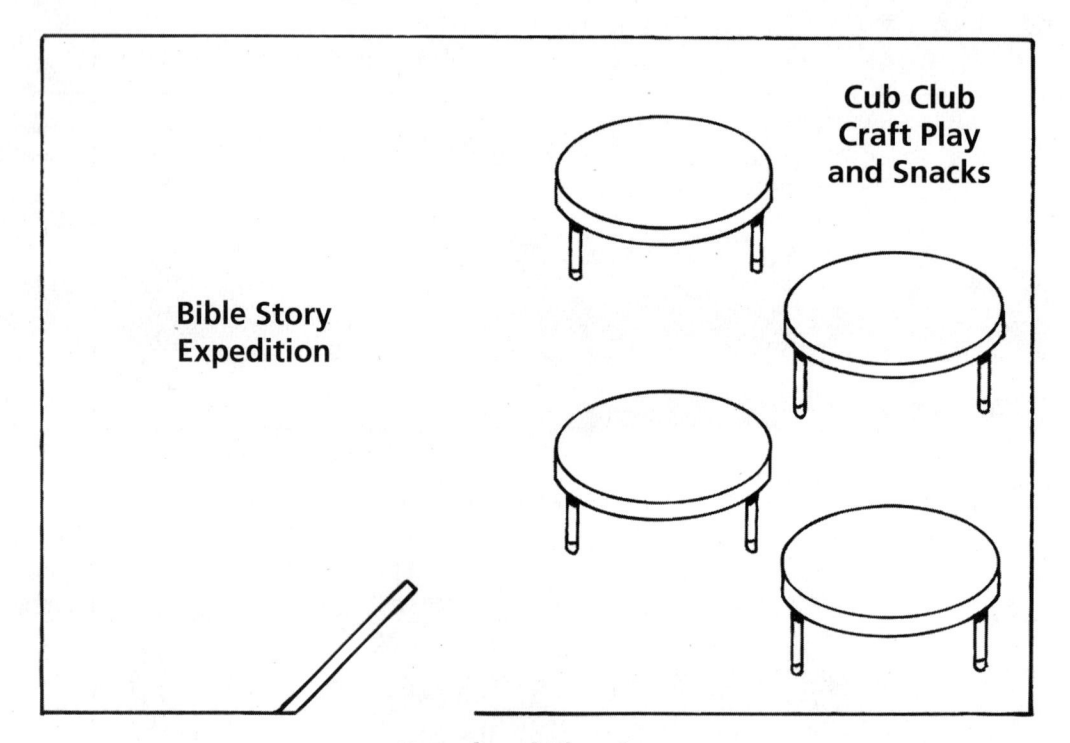

Cub Club Craft Play and Snacks

Bible Story Expedition

Preschool Playtime

OPTIONAL PRESCHOOL ROTATION SCHEDULE

INTRODUCTION

If you have more than twenty-five preschoolers, you might consider having preschoolers rotate to three areas of Lion Cub Club. Form three groups, then simply plug them into the schedule below.

Day 1
Arrive in Lion Cub Club area for Wild Welcome (10 minutes). Then travel to Watering Hole Snacks to make snacks for the entire Serengeti Trek. After making snacks, travel back to the Lion Cub Club room for Bible Story Expedition. Then continue with the schedule below.

Days 2-5
Crew leaders meet preschoolers at Sing & Play Roar with the rest of the children attending Serengeti Trek.

Travel back to Lion Cub Club, and gather all preschoolers together for Wild Welcome and Bible Story Expedition (about 20 minutes total). Then continue with the schedule below. It's important that preschoolers hear the Bible story first before they do Cub Club Craft Play and Preschool Playtime.

Time	Group A Crews_____	Group B Crews_____	Group C Crews_____
20 minutes	*Chadder's Serengeti Trek Adventure* video and Bible Memory Buddies	Cub Club Craft Play	Preschool Playtime
15 minutes	Watering Hole Snacks		
20 minutes	Cub Club Craft Play	Preschool Playtime	*Chadder's Serengeti Trek Adventure* video and Bible Memory Buddies
20 minutes	Preschool Playtime	*Chadder's Serengeti Trek Adventure* video and Bible Memory Buddies	Cub Club Craft Play

Then gather everyone, and grab lion tails to travel to The Mane Event.

- Make sure all the furniture in your room is child-size. If it's too big, it can cause accidents. If you can't get child-size tables and chairs, remove the furniture, and set up work areas on the floor. (Lengths of animal-print cloth taped to the floor work great for this because they indicate special areas for each activity.)
- Set up an eating area in your room. If you'll be using the tables for other activities, you may want to have children eat on cloth that you've placed on the floor.

INTRODUCTION

TREK TIPS

We've suggested plenty of decorating options. You can choose or adapt any or all of the suggestions to fit your room, your time, and your budget. Remember, you will have lots of appealing, eye-catching activities set up each day for preschoolers, so your decorations don't need to be elaborate.

- Stock your room with age-appropriate toys and games. In addition to the supplies listed on pages 17-18, children will enjoy dress-up clothes, a water table, blocks, plastic animals, modeling dough, toy food and dishes, dolls, and stuffed animals.

- On Day 2, hang one of the Operation Kid-to-Kid posters in the Bible Story Expedition area. Then add new posters on Days 3 and 4. These posters make the school-supply project much more real and tangible to preschoolers, who may not realize that kids around the world are a lot alike. (The Operation Kid-to-Kid poster set is available from Group Publishing and your local Christian bookstore.)

- Photocopy the Lion Cub Club sign and arrow (pp. 112-113). Color the sign, and tape it to your meeting-room door. Put up copies of the arrow along the church hallways leading to your room.

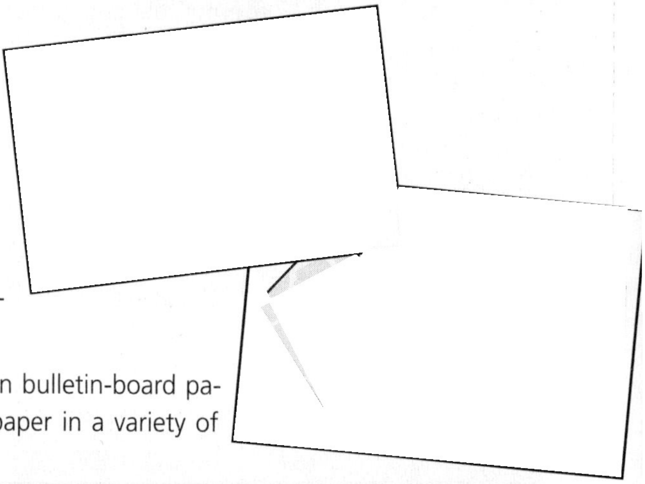

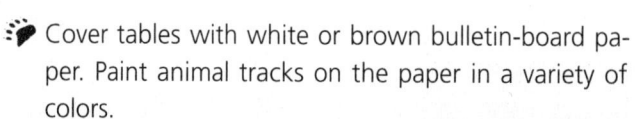

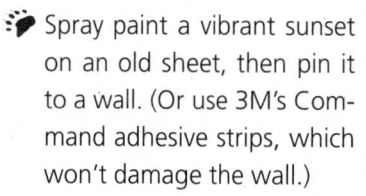

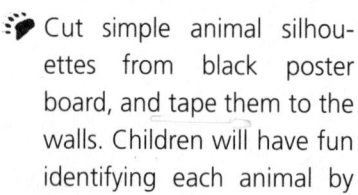

- Use the following suggestions to transform your room for Lion Cub Club:

  - Cover tables with white or brown bulletin-board paper. Paint animal tracks on the paper in a variety of colors.

  - Spray paint a vibrant sunset on an old sheet, then pin it to a wall. (Or use 3M's Command adhesive strips, which won't damage the wall.)

  - Cut simple animal silhouettes from black poster board, and tape them to the walls. Children will have fun identifying each animal by its basic shape—kind of like they do with animal crackers!

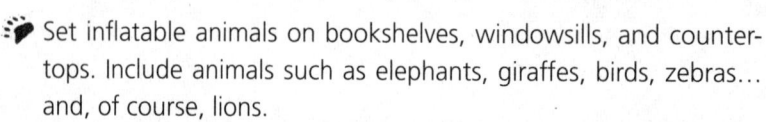

  - Set inflatable animals on bookshelves, windowsills, and countertops. Include animals such as elephants, giraffes, birds, zebras… and, of course, lions.

  - Set out a child-size Jeep for kids to play on. Simply remove the battery to keep this safe and fun for indoors.

LION CUB CLUB BASIC SUPPLIES

Gather the basic supplies listed below, and refer to the activities you've chosen to determine what other supplies you'll need. Then see the list of additional supplies (including the supplies for each option).

- Bible
- *Sing & Play Roar Music* audiocassette or CD*
- cassette player or CD player
- 1 jump-rope or 10-foot length of soft rope per Cub Crew, to use for traveling
- 1 masking-tape roll per crew
- staplers
- paper
- 1 permanent marker per crew
- modeling dough
- crayons
- washable markers
- child-size scissors
- glue sticks
- tacky glue
- paper dessert plates (for holding tacky glue)
- Glue Dots*
- wet wipes (for cleaning children's hands before eating snacks or after making crafts)
- paper towels
- sidewalk chalk
- TV and VCR (or DVD player) for showing the *Chadder's Serengeti Trek Adventure* video
- *Chadder's Serengeti Trek Adventure* video or DVD*
- tic tac drum* or other attention-getting signal
- Baby Buddies poster set (optional)*
- 1 Serengeti Trek name badge per child*
- 1 Cub Club Bible Book per child*
- 1 set of 5 Bible Memory Buddies per child*
- 1 Cub Crew Bag per Cub Crew*
- Bible Story poster set*
- Bible Point poster set (optional)*
- Operation Kid-to-Kid poster set*
- Treasure Verse posters (optional)*

*These items are available from Group Publishing and your local Christian bookstore.

All of these supplies are easy to find... and I'm not lyin'.

INTRODUCTION

TREK TIPS

Attention-getting signals let children know when it's time to stop what they're doing and look at you. You can use the tic tac drum (available from Group Publishing and your local Christian bookstore) or another noisemaker of your choice. The first time that students come to Lion Cub Club, introduce and rehearse your attention-getting signal. Once children are familiar with the signal, regaining their attention will become automatic.

HINTS FROM THE HERD

Preschoolers enjoyed using paint markers for some of the crafts. However, we did find it necessary to cover the tables with newspaper.

TREK TIPS

The Wild Games Leader will be using pool noodles for several games. Check with him or her to see if you can borrow a few for Preschool Playtime on Days 4 and 5.

ADDITIONAL SUPPLIES

Use this as a checklist when you stock your Lion Cub Club room with supplies. **Depending on the activities you choose, you may not need all the supplies listed below.**

Day 1
- ❏ Bible Buddy Drum Kits* (1 per child)
- ❏ brown plastic lacing (24 inches per child)
- ❏ yarn (12 inches per child)
- ❏ Serengeti Trek sticker sheets*
- ❏ red, orange, and yellow tissue paper
- ❏ Bugles snacks (1 or 2 per child)
- ❏ black or brown construction paper (1 sheet per child)
- ❏ gel pens or white crayons (for writing names on the black paper)
- ❏ plastic tarp
- ❏ paper bowls (1 per child)
- ❏ pitcher of water
- ❏ 1 sheet of white poster board
- ❏ black crepe-paper streamers (about 1 foot per child)
- ❏ double-sided tape

Day 2
- ❏ Talk Talk Drum Kits* (1 per child)
- ❏ yellow yarn (about 2 feet per child)
- ❏ yellow construction paper (about ¼ sheet per child)
- ❏ brown construction paper (about ¼ sheet per child)
- ❏ yellow rickrack (optional)
- ❏ dot stickers (3 dots per child)
- ❏ dinner-size paper plates (1 per child)
- ❏ toy telephones, cell phones, or walkie-talkies
- ❏ small square box (like an empty tissue box)
- ❏ craft paper or plain wrapping paper

Day 3
- ❏ Wildlife Photo Frame Kits* (1 per child)
- ❏ red, yellow, and orange tissue paper
- ❏ blocks (about 10 per crew)
- ❏ wide craft sticks (4 per crew)
- ❏ African animal picture books
- ❏ watercolor paints and paintbrushes
- ❏ white crayons
- ❏ white paper plates
- ❏ Serengeti Trek sticker sheets*
- ❏ red and orange crepe-paper streamers (1 roll of each)

Day 4
- ❏ paper lunch sacks (1 per crew)
- ❏ plastic Easter eggs (5 per crew)
- ❏ chenille wires (2 per crew)
- ❏ small stones (1 per crew)
- ❏ scraps of white cloth (1 scrap per crew)
- ❏ glitter
- ❏ Wild Wobblers* (1 per child)
- ❏ round Chinet paper plates (1 per child)
- ❏ heart stickers (1 or 2 per child)
- ❏ pool noodles
- ❏ candy or stickers

Day 5
- ❏ Lug's Water Blaster Kits* (1 per child)
- ❏ hole punch
- ❏ cups of water
- ❏ black chenille wires (about 4 per child)
- ❏ paper plates (1 per child)
- ❏ Serengeti Trek stickers*
- ❏ colorful crepe-paper streamers
- ❏ uncooked beans (1 handful per child)
- ❏ black crepe-paper streamers
- ❏ playground balls
- ❏ pool noodles
- ❏ 1-gallon resealable plastic bags (1 per crew)

*These items are available from Group Publishing and your local Christian bookstore.

SERENGETI TREK SAFETY TIPS

- Remove any small toys or objects that the children could choke on or swallow. It's wise to remove anything smaller than a fifty-cent piece just in case you have children who are younger than three years old wandering through.

- If you take the preschoolers outdoors, keep them within a confined space. If your church doesn't have a fenced-in area, you may want to mark off an area with a rope border or cones, or show kids natural borderlines, such as trees or a sidewalk.

- Make sure all the children stay together when they leave the room to go to other activities. Children in each Cub Crew can hold on to a rope that their Cub Crew Leader holds one end of. Or the children can hold hands to make a Serengeti snake!

- After Serengeti Trek each day, release preschoolers only to parents or caregivers to ensure that the children don't get lost.

Don't forget to make your Lion Cub Club the safest place this side of Mount Kilimanjaro!

WHAT'S A CUB CREW?

TREK TIPS

Cub Crew Leaders will have a much easier time if you include three-year-olds, four-year-olds, and five-year-olds in each group. Four- and five-year-olds will be able to do many of the activities themselves, leaving the Cub Crew Leaders free to help the three-year-olds.

Cub Crews are small groups of preschoolers who participate together in Serengeti Trek each day. Each Cub Crew consists of up to five children and one adult or teenage Cub Crew Leader. With one leader shepherding five children, you can be assured that your preschoolers will get lots of attention and discipline issues will decrease. Use the developmental information below to guide you as you work with preschoolers at Serengeti Trek.

We're three years old. We've just learned how to play together, and we're still learning how to share and take turns. It may be a little hard for us to change activities, so give us plenty of warning ahead of time.

We're generally happy and sometimes even silly, but we may be a little shy about trying new things. We enjoy playing games that involve moving and jumping around, but we may tire more quickly than our older playmates.

We'll probably need a little help to complete some of the activities, especially those that involve squeezing glue bottles or cutting with scissors.

HINTS FROM THE HERD

We found that the Cub Crew Leaders and the children benefited when we assigned Assistant Cub Crew Leaders to children who were more active or who had difficulty staying with their Cub Crews. Assistant crew leaders can be teenagers or middle schoolers.

We're four years old. We're full of imagination and excitement. We love to use our imaginations in make-believe play and art activities. We like to use loud voices and big movements. You may need to remind us to play quietly at Lion Cub Club. We enjoy listening to Bible stories and answering interesting questions such as "What sound does an elephant make?"

We're five years old. We love to help our Cub Crew Leaders and our other leaders. If you notice us helping, please tell us thank you.

We're proud of the things we can do, but we're also sensitive. Other children may hurt our feelings by blurting out reactions to things we do. We're improving in our coordination. We can cut with scissors and color between the lines. We're also pretty good at throwing and catching balls.

We're wild about God!

Permission to photocopy this page from Group's Serengeti Trek: Lion Cub Club Preschool Director Manual granted for local church use. Copyright © Group Publishing, Inc. P.O. Box 481, Loveland, CO 80539
www.groupvbs.com

Dear Parents:

We're so glad you've signed up your child for a busy week at Serengeti Trek. This VBS program is a wonderful way to help your little one explore God's love in new ways.

You'll notice that things at Serengeti Trek are…well, a little different than you might be used to. For one thing, preschoolers will be in small, mixed-age groups with other young children three- through five-years-old. These small groups, called Cub Crews, are led by adults or teenagers who love children and love the Lord. Cub Crews are an important part of Serengeti Trek! But you still might have some doubts…

"My five-year-old will be bored with all of these little kids." Five-year-olds play an important role in their Cub Crews. They become the "big kids" who can cut with more accuracy, glue more easily, and (gasp!) even write their names! Younger children will *love* being with your child and will show their affection generously. All this admiration is wonderful for your child's self-esteem and allows him or her to serve younger children in hands-on, practical ways.

"My three-year-old will get hurt by the older kids." Actually, the younger children will be loved, served, and doted on by the older children in their Cub Crews. Plus, in a mixed-age small group, the Cub Crew Leader has much more time to spend one-on-one with your child. And you can be sure that the activities are all specially designed for mixed-age groups, so younger children won't be in over their heads.

"My child won't come if she can't be with her friend." While it's true that your child may not be with his or her very best friend, there will be opportunities to make many new friends. Studies show that children learn as much—or more—when they're linked with kids of different ages. If your child really needs the security of a familiar face, we can most likely pair him or her with one special friend.

Millions of children have experienced this multi-age "family" approach at Group's VBS, with surprise and delight at the outcome. Children's ministry experts agree that combining ages has numerous benefits: teaching children to work together, experiencing what it means to be a family, and serving others in love, for example. However, the most important factor in making this program a success is your attitude. If your child has doubts, reassure him or her that this is a wonderful opportunity to try something new. Your support will speak volumes to the children we're serving.

We look forward to ministering to your child at Serengeti Trek!

Lion Cub Club Director

Permission to photocopy this page from Group's Serengeti Trek: Lion Cub Club Preschool Director Manual granted for local church use. Copyright © Group Publishing, Inc. P.O. Box 481, Loveland, CO 80539. www.groupvbs.com

WHAT'S OPERATION KID-TO-KID™?

TREK TIPS

You may be used to having children bring money for a missions offering or toward a missions project. However, most children don't understand the value of money—it's not a tangible "need" for them. Therefore, it's difficult to make a concrete connection to how they're really making a difference in the life of another child. On the other hand, children are familiar with Bible picture books. Kids can easily identify with this need! We've designed this missions project to have a big impact—on the kids who give and on the kids who receive!

MORE THAN AN OFFERING

We know that today's kids are service-minded and want to make a difference, both globally and within their communities. From customer feedback, we also know that VBS directors want kids to give more than money. They want kids to give something that is meaningful and tangible—something that will meet the needs of children across the world. That's why we developed Operation Kid-to-Kid! Over the years, Operation Kid-to-Kid has become one of the largest child-to-child service outreach programs!

> Operation Kid-to-Kid is an international missions project that allows hundreds of thousands of kids in North America to serve children around the world. What a great way to *reach* out with God's love!

THE GREATEST GIFT

Founded in 1950, World Vision is a Christian relief and development organization, serving the world's poorest children and families in nearly one hundred countries. International Bible Society has been reaching people with God's Word for nearly two hundred years. By partnering with IBS and World Vision, we want to give the kids at Serengeti Trek the opportunity to share God's love with children across the globe. Just think: When your church participates, you'll join other Serengeti Trek programs, and together you could contribute over *one million* African Bible books and two hundred thousand school supply kits to needy children! Operation Kid-to-Kid is a practical, meaningful way for kids to demonstrate God's love through giving and service. (For more information about Operation Kid-to-Kid, check out www.ok2k.org.)

> Kids take pride in *this* missions project! Collecting offerings doesn't connect with kids in a tangible way. However, children *do* understand the value of having school supplies of their very own.

HOW YOUR KIDS CAN HELP

Each child will find a copy of *A Time for Everything* inside his or her Cub Club Bible Book. This simple book is designed specifically to help kids in Africa deal with the grief and loss many of them face daily. Due to the AIDS crisis in Africa, countless children are orphaned each year. An interactive book like *A Time for Everything* (based on Ecclesiastes 3) can help these children by giving them opportunities to process their emotions. International Bible Society has partnered with World Vision to create a book that gives orphans the hope of God's love. People who work with children in Africa have specially created this colorful book. By sending these Bible books to children in Africa, the kids at your Serengeti Trek can share God's love!

But *A Time for Everything* isn't all you'll send! Starting on Day 2, kids will bring in specific school supplies from the handout on page 25. As the mountain of school supplies grows, kids will discover that they can accomplish big things—especially when they work together! On Day 5, you'll guide each crew in creating a special school supply kit. They'll drop their *Time for Everything* books into the school supply kits so the recipients can share God's Word with their family and friends.

At the last Mane Event (on Day 5), you'll present the school supply kits as an offering. This is a powerful, moving ceremony. Kids and leaders will be amazed as they see just how many beautiful new items they'll send to Africa. It's a very concrete way for kids to learn that it's easy to see God's love grow. (And it's just one more way to add to their Daily Challenge accomplishments.)

IT'S AS EASY AS 1, 2, 3!

1. Hang up one Operation Kid-to-Kid poster on Day 2. Explain the importance of school supplies, and remind kids that they can help kids in Africa with this program. (Operation Kid-to-Kid posters are available from Group Publishing or your local Christian bookstore.)

2. Set eight boxes in your Bible Story Expedition area. Tape a picture of a school supply to each box so children know where to place their items.

3. Starting on Day 2, ask who has brought in their Operation Kid-to-Kid items. Applaud for kids as they bring the items forward. (Work with your director to provide additional supplies since not every child will be able to bring in an item.)

IMPORTANT SPECIFICS

Since World Vision has tested this program, there are specific guidelines which *must* be followed to ensure that your school packs are delivered to the children who need them most.

- **All items must be new and in their original packaging.** The children receiving these items seldom get anything new. Leaving items in the original packaging so children can unwrap them will create more excitement for the recipients.

- **Each kit must include precisely the same items.** This way, foreign customs officials examining the crates containing thousands of kits will not prevent or delay delivery. For example, all the pencils must be painted yellow, not different colors. The crayons must be in boxes of twenty-four, not in boxes of sixteen or forty-eight. Providing identical items also prevents some children from being disappointed because they didn't receive as much as other children.

- **Each set of school supplies must be placed in a one-gallon resealable plastic bag.** These bags allow foreign customs officials to see clearly what each pack contains. They also become handy storage units (and can even hold fresh water) for the recipients.

- **Only place school supply items and the *Time for Everything* book inside the bags.** Some children may ask if they can add candy, stickers, or toys to the school packs. Commend kids for their generosity, but explain that children who didn't get such treasures in their packs would feel bad.

INTRODUCTION

TREK TIPS

On page 25, you'll find a photocopiable letter explaining this program to parents. Although the Mane Event Leader will photocopy and distribute these letters to elementary kids on Day 1, preschoolers will discuss them in the less-distracting setting of Lion Cub Club. Plus, you'll want to have extras on hand for kids who come later in the week. We discovered that everyone wanted to take part in this missions project!

HINTS FROM THE HERD

Preschoolers really got into this Operation Kid-to-Kid project. Little ones felt so proud about bringing in their pencils and crayons to share, and parents commented that their preschoolers were excited to participate with the "big kids." By allowing preschoolers to participate in this hands-on missions project, you're setting the stage for a lifetime of serving!

HINTS FROM THE HERD

We started to get worried at our field test when it seemed as if we wouldn't have enough items to create every kit. But on the last day, kids and parents brought in more than enough supplies! Every crew made a kit, and we even had supplies left over. They did it!

INTRODUCTION

TREK TIPS

Since there are eight items in the school kit, some kids will need to bring more than one. We suggest "pairing up" less expensive items, such as the eraser and the ruler or the pencil sharpener and the crayons.

Wow! Look what kids have done through Operation Kid-to-Kid™!

- **1998** Kids in North America sent more than 91,000 school supply kits to children around the world.
- **1999** Children involved in Operation Kid-to-Kid sent approximately 400,000 Spanish translations of the Gospel of John to Spanish-speaking children around the world.
- **2000** Film Crews at Group's HolyWord Studios created more than 100,000 care kits that were distributed in countries such as Thailand, Vietnam, and Albania.
- **2001** Cool Crews who took part in Polar Expedition sent more than 380,000 gift boxes to needy children across the globe!
- **2002** It's estimated that children in North America sent more than 1 million Bible coloring books to orphans in Russia and Romania! Wow!
- **2003** Kids at Group's SCUBA VBS sent more than 200,000 pairs of shoes and over 100,000 pairs of socks to orphans around the world. (We think that's *shoe*-per!)
- **2004** The numbers aren't in, but as this manual is being written, kids at Lava Lava Island are sending nearly 1 million Spanish Bible books to kids in Spanish-speaking countries.
- **2005** Who knows what we can do?

Thanks for joining us in this exciting, world-changing project!

Dear Parent,

Group's **SERENGETI TREK** is partnering with World Vision (an international relief organization) and International Bible Society to provide school supply kits for children in Africa. These children have been deprived of basic supplies needed for learning. You and your child can help needy children learn and grow through a small contribution.

Each Cub Crew of about five preschoolers is on a special mission to put together a school supply kit made up of the items pictured here. Crew members work together to choose the items each person will donate. The one or two items checked (or circled) is what your child volunteered to donate.

Each kit must include precisely the same items. This way, foreign customs officials will not delay or prevent delivery. For example, the crayons must be 24-count, not 16 or 48. This also prevents children from being disappointed because they didn't receive as much as others. Thanks for remembering that as you purchase the items.

Items must be new and in their original packaging. The children receiving these kits seldom get anything new. Leaving items in their original packaging will create more excitement for them as they open their kits. (Product brand doesn't matter. The items pictured are simply examples of what you might send.)

Children must bring their items to their Cub Crew Leaders by the last day of Serengeti Trek. If you are unable to donate the item(s) checked, please circle this paragraph, and have your child return this sheet to his or her Cub Crew Leader.

Thanks for participating in Operation Kid-to-Kid!

Please have your child bring in the checked item(s):

- ❏ 24-pack of regular-size crayons 
- ❏ package of 7 or 8 yellow pencils (without designs) 
- ❏ eraser (pink gum type) 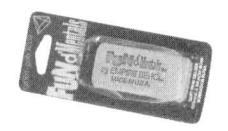
- ❏ pencil sharpener 
- ❏ two 6x9-inch steno pads 
- ❏ package of 10 or 12 ballpoint pens 
- ❏ 12-inch ruler with metric markings

Permission to photocopy this handout from Group's Serengeti Trek: Lion Cub Club Preschool Director Manual granted for local church use. Copyright © Group Publishing, Inc., P.O. Box 481, Loveland, CO 80539. www.groupvbs.com

WHAT'S THE DAILY CHALLENGE™?

DAILY CHALLENGE™

Of course you want kids to come to Serengeti Trek and learn about God's love. But imagine how life-changing it would be if kids took what they'd learned and applied it *right away* to daily life so they could "leave" a little bit of God's love in the lives of others.

That's where the Daily Challenge comes in! It's as easy as 1, 2, 3!

1. During Cub Club Craft Play, preschoolers will look over that day's Daily Challenges, found on the back of each day's Bible Activity Page in the Cub Club Bible Book. Crew leaders will help children choose which challenge they'll do at home after they leave VBS for the day.

2. During Watering Hole Snacks, crews will talk about the Daily Challenges again. Crew leaders will remind children of their Daily Challenges and encourage preschoolers to carry out this important mission! At the end of the day, children will take home the Daily Challenge with their Bible Activity Page.

3. Starting on Day 2, when kids come to Sing & Play Roar, the Sing & Play Roar Leader will ask them to gather with their crews and talk about how they carried out the Daily Challenges. As preschoolers share, they'll each take an acacia leaf from the Crew Bag and hand it to the crew leader. On the Sing & Play Roar Leader's cue, crew leaders will come to the front and press the leaves onto a large acacia tree.

What a fun way to "leave" a little love!

IMPORTANT!

Encourage kids to practice what they're learning just for the joy of serving Jesus! Do not offer bribes or incentives to entice kids to complete their Daily Challenges. We discovered that children were intrinsically motivated—they were excited about choosing a Daily Challenge and living it out.

Kids receive so many cool things at VBS. Don't fall into the trap of thinking kids won't carry out their Daily Challenges unless they get something. They do get something—the joy of giving and seeing God's love grow through their acts of kindness!

SERENGETI TREK IS CRAWLING WITH NEW FRIENDS!

Each day at Serengeti Trek, kids meet an adorable buddy who reminds them of the day's Bible Point. They're Bible Memory Buddies®! We'll let our fun friends speak for themselves.

I'm Zach! Zebras know other zebras by their stripe pattern. I'll remind kids to know God!

It's me... Roary! Lions talk to one another really loudly! I want kids to talk to God!

Hey, friends, it's **Elaine the Crane!** You can tell a crowned crane is talking by its unique voice. I help kids remember to tell about God.

My name's Lug, and like all elephants, I'm a hard worker. I'll help kids remember to work hard and cheerfully for God.

Gigi here. My long neck helps me reach the tops of trees. I want kids to love God because he reached down and loved us.

To help kids remember these important Bible truths, the Chadder's Adventure Theater Leader will give each child a Bible Memory Buddy every day to keep in his or her Bible Buddy Drum (an awesome craft that kids make on Day 1). And each Buddy has the Treasure Verse inscribed on it. Kids will *love* collecting these buddies! And you'll be amazed at how the Bible Memory Buddies help kids apply Bible truths to everyday life.

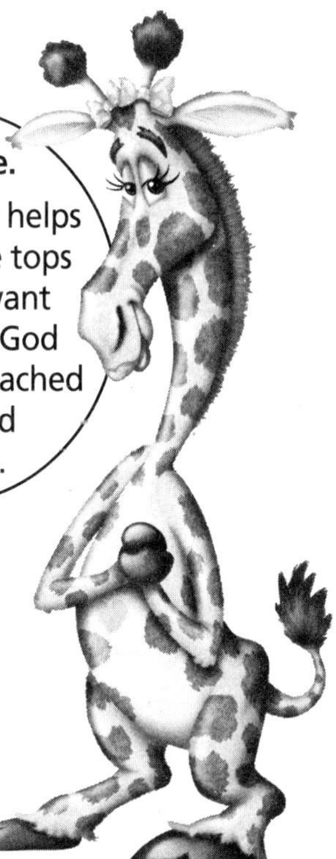

WWW.GROUPVBS.COM

LION CUB CLUB
PRESCHOOL DIRECTOR MANUAL

DAY 1

BIBLE POINT:
Know God.

BIBLE STORY:
Gideon defeats the Midianites (Judges 7:1-22).

TREASURE VERSE:
"I know the greatness of the Lord" (Psalm 135:5).

When we find Gideon in Judges 6:11, he certainly seems an unlikely hero. His people, the Israelites, have turned from God to worship idols. His land is overrun with ruthless invaders from Midian, who send the people into hiding. And Gideon? He's cowering in a wine press, threshing his wheat in secret. Is this really the man God would use to defeat an entire *army* of Midianites? It seems as if Gideon needed a reminder of who God really is.

In Judges 6, Gideon met the God his people had forgotten, and through a series of miraculous tests, God became very real to him. He discovered the power and faithfulness of a mighty God. Even as he faced a seemingly invincible army, Gideon put his complete faith in God. And because Gideon knew and trusted God, he successfully led an army of three hundred men against an enemy of thousands. Gideon's life was changed because he knew God. More important, it seems that his heart was changed.

Like the Israelites, kids today often forget the amazing things God has done in their lives. The distractions of school, friendships, sports, and clubs crowd out the importance of a life-changing relationship with God. Sometimes kids feel like the world is against them and God is nowhere to be found. The kids who come to your VBS may need to "meet" God and discover who he really is. For some kids, this will be a first-time introduction (how exciting!). For others it will be an eye-opening reminder of how awesome our God is. Use the activities in this lesson to help kids know the faithful, mighty God who loves them.

Because I know God, I will

- discover what it means to follow God,
- explore ways to share God's love with others,
- make God part of my everyday life, and
- celebrate God.

LION CUB CLUB SCHEDULE

DAY 1

LOCATION	ACTIVITY	MINUTES	WHAT CHILDREN WILL DO	SUPPLIES
Lion Cub Club	Wild Welcome	up to 10	Meet their classmates and Cub Crew Leaders, practice the attention-getting signal, and sing a welcoming song.	Serengeti Trek name badges, markers, crew signs, ropes for traveling in groups, Bible Story posters, tic tac drum
Watering Hole Snacks or Lion Cub Club	Watering Hole Snacks Service	up to 25	Make Gideon's Trail Mix to remember that Gideon knew God.	Supplies provided by the Watering Hole Snacks Leader
Lion Cub Club	Bible Story Expedition	up to 15	Discover how Gideon knew that God would help him defeat a mighty enemy.	Bible
Lion Cub Club	Cub Club Craft Play	up to 20	**Option 1: Bible Buddy Drums**—Create fun "homes" for their Bible Memory Buddies.	Bible Buddy Drum Kits, Serengeti Trek sticker sheets, plastic lacing, yarn
			Option 2: Golden Horns and Glowing Torches—Glue Bugles and flames to pictures of Gideon's army, and talk about the Daily Challenges.	Cub Club Bible Books; red, orange, and yellow tissue paper pieces; glue; Bugles snacks; paper dessert plates
			Option 3: Flaming Torches—Make flaming torches to remind them of Gideon's victory.	Black or brown construction paper; red, yellow, and orange tissue paper; gel pens or white crayons; stapler
			Option 4: Water Drinking—Pretend to be the men that Gideon chose to serve in his army.	Plastic tarp, paper bowls, pitchers of water
Lion Cub Club	Chadder's Adventure Theater	up to 15	Watch as Chadder Chipmunk travels to Africa and chooses a guide to lead his expedition.	TV/VCR or TV/DVD player, *Chadder's Serengeti Trek Adventure* video
Watering Hole Snacks or Lion Cub Club	Watering Hole Snacks	up to 15	Eat snacks and get to know their Cub Crew members.	Snacks made earlier, paper towels, cups of water, wet wipes
Lion Cub Club or outside	Preschool Playtime	up to 20	**Option 1: Gideon's Torch Relay**—Travel with Gideon's torch and call out, "Know God."	Torch made in Cub Club Craft Play
			Option 2: Who Will Join the Army?—Pretend to join Gideon's army.	Torch made in Cub Club Craft Play
			Option 3: Pin the Stripes on the Zebra—Put stripes on Zach the Zebra.	Outline picture of a zebra, poster board, strips of black crepe-paper streamers, double-sided tape
			Option 4: Free Play—Enjoy free play outdoors or in the classroom.	Playground equipment, various outdoor toys, or classroom toys
Lion Cub Club	Bible Memory Buddies	up to 10	Play a guessing game, and receive a Bible Memory Buddy named Zach the Zebra.	Day 1 Bible Point poster, Zach Bible Memory Buddies
The Mane Event	The Mane Event	up to 20	Sing songs, and watch an experiment that reminds them that Gideon knew God.	Supplies provided by The Mane Event Leader

LION CUB CLUB PREPARATIONS

DAY 1

Before the children arrive:

- Set out blocks, stuffed animals, animal and African-themed books, or other classroom toys for the children to play with when they arrive.

- Cut rope into 10-foot lengths for Cub Crews to hold on to when traveling from one place to another. (We'll call these "lion tails"!)

- Consult with the Watering Hole Snacks Leader about how the preschoolers will prepare today's snacks, and ask the Watering Hole Snacks Leader how you and your Cub Crew Leaders can help during snack preparation. Agree on a location (your room or the Watering Hole Snacks area) and a time to prepare the snacks. If you'll make the snacks in the Lion Cub Club room, set up a snack preparation area.

- Choose the Cub Club Craft Play activities you'll use, photocopy the instructions, and collect and prepare the supplies. If the activity is a craft, it's a good idea to make a sample craft to show children what they'll be making. Set up each station as shown, and cover the supplies with a sheet so they won't be a distraction to busy preschoolers.

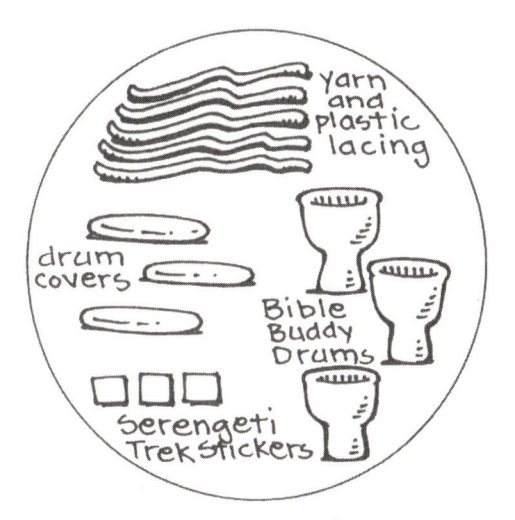

Bible Buddy Drums — yarn and plastic lacing, drum covers, Bible Buddy Drums, Serengeti Trek Stickers

Golden Horns and Glowing Torches — red, orange, yellow tissue paper, bag of Bugles, dessert plates, glue

Flaming Torches — stapler, black construction paper, red, orange, yellow tissue paper, gel pens or white crayons

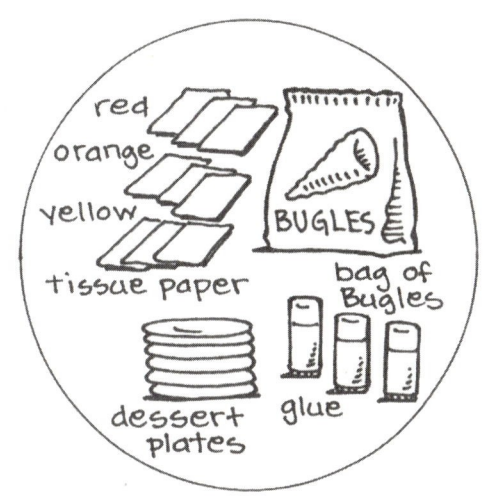

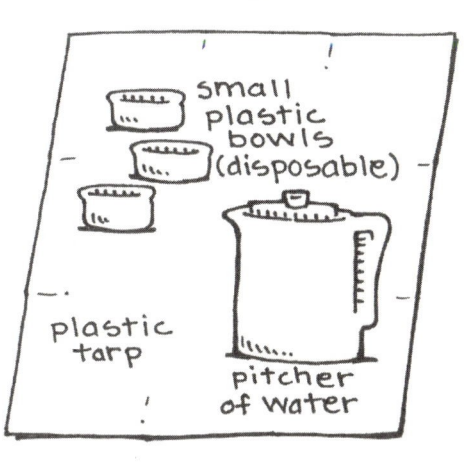

Water Drinking — small plastic bowls (disposable), plastic tarp, pitcher of water

---

HINTS FROM THE HERD

Preschoolers looked so cute traveling from place to place holding on to their lion tails. The ropes are used in some of the Preschool Playtime activities, so make sure the crews always travel with them.

HINTS FROM THE HERD

We set out glue bottles for the "Golden Horns and Glowing Torches" activity, only to discover that preschoolers used way too much glue. During the second rotation, we squirted a small puddle of glue on a paper dessert plate and directed kids to simply dip the Bugles and paper in the glue. It worked great!

TREK TIPS

Don't feel like you need to save the Safari Sing-Along songs until the end of the day. We used them whenever we needed a time-filler! Familiarize yourself with these simple tunes so you're prepared to lead children as they wash their hands, while you're waiting in line at the bathroom, or if you happen to have a few minutes after an activity.

WWW.GroupVBS.com 31

DAY 1

TREK TIPS

Check with your Serengeti Trek Director to be sure that he or she has recruited a helper for preschool registration; make sure the helper knows to put children into mixed-age groups. Let the helper check in the children so you will be available to greet and guide children to their Cub Crews. Communication with your registration workers, Cub Crew Leaders, and Assistant Cub Crew Leaders is essential for getting off to a good start. *Make sure you have a foolproof plan so preschoolers and their caretakers know that the kids are welcome and safe.*

HINTS FROM THE HERD

For some of your preschoolers, this may be the first time they've been in a group setting away from home. You may see some separation anxiety expressed by crying, clinging to parents, or acting out in other ways. Try to arrange to have a few extra adults on hand to help settle the children down.

- Hang up the Day 1 Bible Story poster on a wall near your Bible Story Expedition area. You'll add new posters each day, so try to find an area where all the posters can easily fit.

- Remember that preschoolers will spend their opening time today at Lion Cub Club rather than at Sing & Play Roar. This will allow time for the children to meet their Cub Crew Leaders and will ensure that you're ready for Watering Hole Snacks Service. On Days 2 through 5, you and your Cub Crew Leaders will meet the preschoolers in the Sing & Play Roar area.

- Get registration materials from the Serengeti Trek Director. The director will have preregistered the preschoolers and assigned them to Cub Crews. Be sure to get extra forms for any walk-in students.

- You'll probably need a volunteer to staff the preschool registration table for fifteen to twenty minutes after your program begins to assist latecomers. Have the volunteer help children find the right Cub Crews.

- Give each Cub Crew Leader a large sign that has the crew name on it as well as a related picture of a Serengeti animal or bird that kids will recognize. Have the crew leaders wait in the registration area and hold up the signs where parents and other caregivers can see them. Some preschoolers can't tell you their names yet, so make sure you have a fail-safe plan to get name tags on children before they have left their parents and entered the Lion Cub Club.

- Give each Cub Crew Leader five Serengeti Trek name badges, a roll of masking tape, a permanent marker, five Cub Club Bible Books, and a rope (about 10 feet long) to use as a lion tail. Cub Crew Leaders can keep the items in their Cub Crew bags. Depending on the number of children in each Cub Crew, you can adjust the amount of supplies you give to each crew leader.

WILD WELCOME

(up to 10 minutes)

As the preschoolers arrive, greet each child with an enthusiastic smile, and lead each child to his or her Cub Crew Leader. This one-on-one connection is a great way to start the week. It gives the parents a chance to meet the Cub Crew Leaders so parents will know who their children are talking about all week! As you greet the children, ask them their names. Have each child's Cub Crew Leader use a marker to write the child's name on a name badge and on the Cub Crew sign.

Tell the children that you're glad they've come to explore Lion Cub Club, and invite them to play with the toys you've set out.

When everyone has arrived, let the Cub Crew Leaders

DAY 1

help the children put away the toys and then join you on the floor. Be sure the children are sitting with their Cub Crews.

Shake the tic tac drum to get the children's attention, then **SAY:** Welcome! I'm (your name), **and I'm the Lion Cub Club Director at Serengeti Trek. Are you ready for our Serengeti Trek? The Serengeti is in a far-away country where tall grasses grow and animals roam the land. Many people travel there to go on a safari, or journey, to see the animals. We're going to have a great time this week! Every day when you come to Lion Cub Club, we're going to pretend we're doing fun things on our Serengeti Trek. We'll have special activities, see interesting animals, and learn about God.**

Be sure preschoolers know your name too!

Today we're going to learn what it means to 📖 know God. Knowing God means that we can count on him to help us because he's a great God! Each time you hear someone say "know God," you'll say "Wow!" Let's practice: I 📖 know God. Lead the children in saying "Wow!" Demonstrate how to put your fists near your chin, then fling your fingers out when you say "Wow!" in a loud whisper.

WELCOME SONG

While you're at Lion Cub Club, you'll be traveling with other children in your Cub Crews. Sometimes we'll do things together with all the preschoolers, and sometimes you'll get to do things with just the children in your Cub Crew.

Your Cub Crew Leaders and I want you to know how very happy we are that you're here today, and we want you to help us sing about it.

Have the children sing the welcoming song "I'm So Glad" to the tune of "Ten Little Indians." Lead the children in greeting their friends and doing the motions.

I'm so glad my friends are here. *(Shake hands with a friend.)*

I'm so glad my friends are here. *(Shake hands with a friend.)*

I'm so glad my friends are here *(shake hands with a friend)*

At Ser-en-ge-ti Trek!

Roar!

I'm so glad my friends are here. *(Shake hands with a friend.)*

I'm so glad my friends are here. *(Shake hands with a friend.)*

I'm so glad my friends are here *(shake hands with a friend)*

At Ser-en-ge-ti Trek!

Roar!

SAY: God gave each of you a special person to care for you this week—your Cub Crew Leader. Let's have all the Cub Crew Leaders stand up. If you need help with anything, your Cub Crew Leader will help you. Now take a minute to meet the other members of your Cub Crew. Have the Cub Crew Leaders sit with their crew members and let each child tell his or her name. Then direct the crew leaders to shake each child's hand and say, "Welcome, [child's name]. I'm glad to know you!" After a few minutes, shake the tic tac drum to get the attention of the children.

HINTS FROM THE HERD

Names are important to young children! Be sure the children know your name and the names of their Cub Crew Leaders. Encourage the crew leaders to learn—and use—the names of the children in their Cub Crews.

HINTS FROM THE HERD

Children love listening for the daily Bible Point. Watch their enthusiasm (and listening skills) grow throughout the week. Make sure more emphasis is put on saying the point than on the response.

TREK TIPS

Once kids are familiar with this simple song, feel free to change the motions each day. Instead of shaking hands, children can give high fives or hugs. Or have children suggest different animals to imitate instead of saying "Roar!" at the end of the song.

DAY 1

HINTS FROM THE HERD

This transition turned out to be a perfect time to let kids use the restroom and wash their hands before preparing the snacks.

On the count of three, I want you to tell me your Cub Crew Leader's name. Are you ready? 1…2…3! Repeat this a couple of times, and encourage the children to say the crew leaders' names louder each time. The repetition will help the children remember the crew leaders' names. Shake your tic tac drum.

SNEAKY LIONS

Attention everyone! Sometimes I'll need to get your attention so everyone can hear what to do next. This is my special drum called a tic tac drum. Shake the tic tac drum again. **When I shake the tic tac drum, it means that I need your attention. When you hear the tic tac drum, I want you all to stop what you're doing and listen carefully.**

Give each crew leader a 10-foot length of rope. Explain that this is like a lion tail that children will hold on to when they travel from one activity to another.

SAY: Let's play a game and pretend to be lion cubs sneaking around in the tall grasses on the Serengeti plain. Crawl on all fours and sneak around until you hear the tic tac drum, then crawl over to your Cub Crew and hold on to the lion tail. Repeat the exercise several times, then **SAY: I'm so proud of how quickly you can find your Cub Crews. Now let's all get ready to begin our service for the Watering Hole Snacks!**

We're going to travel together like a family of lions. Hold on to the lion tail. Have the Cub Crew members hold on to their lion tails. **The head of the lion family is your Cub Crew Leader. Make sure you always hold on tight to your lion tail while you travel from place to place.**

The first thing we need to do today is make snacks for everyone who will be with us at Serengeti Trek. Your Cub Crew Leaders will take you to Watering Hole Snacks. Hold on to your lion tails, and let's travel over to Watering Hole Snacks—here we go!

WATERING HOLE SNACKS SERVICE

DAY 1

(up to 25 minutes)

TREK TIPS
While preschoolers are looking at all the snacks they've made, you may want to count the number of snacks and announce the number to your preschoolers. The little ones will be amazed at the big things they can do!

Today the preschoolers will prepare snacks for everyone at Watering Hole Snacks. If you've decided to prepare the snacks in your classroom, the Watering Hole Snacks Leader will come in to help your preschoolers complete this project. If the Watering Hole Snacks Leader hasn't arrived yet, send one of the Cub Crew Leaders to tell the Watering Hole Snacks Leader that you're ready. If you've arranged for the preschoolers to go to the Watering Hole Snacks area to prepare the snacks, send one of the Cub Crew Leaders ahead to let the Watering Hole Snacks Leader know that the kids are coming. When the crew leader returns, have the children gather in their crews and hold hands or hold on to the lion tails as they travel to the Watering Hole Snacks area.

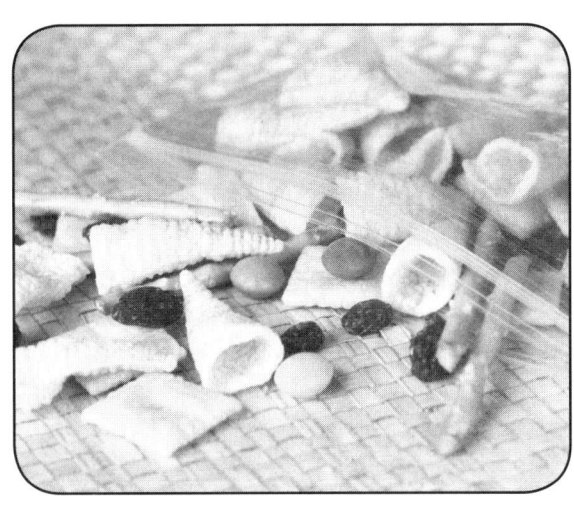

SAY: I'd like you to meet (name of Watering Hole Snacks Leader), **our Watering Hole Snacks Leader. [Name] is going to help us make some yummy treats that we can share with everyone at Serengeti Trek!**

After you've introduced the Watering Hole Snacks Leader, he or she will tell the children about the Gideon's Trail Mix that the kids will be making, show the children where to wash their hands, and then help kids prepare the snacks. The Watering Hole Snacks Leader will assign specific tasks to the children and the Cub Crew Leaders.

After the children have prepared the snacks, set aside enough snacks for all your preschoolers. Be sure you have water, cups, and paper towels or napkins, too. The Watering Hole Snacks Leader will serve the rest of the snacks to older children later in the day. If you have plenty of Cub Crew Leaders, have one or two of them help the Watering Hole Snacks Leader take the snacks to serving tables. Have the other Cub Crew Leaders use wet wipes or paper towels to help clean the children's hands and the snack preparation area.

When everything is cleaned up and all the Cub Crew Leaders have finished with their tasks, shake the tic tac drum, and help the children gather in their Cub Crews.

SAY: Good job finding your Cub Crews—and good job making those snacks! We'll get to eat our snacks a little later. Right now, we're going to do some other fun things, starting with an exciting Bible story. Remember to stay with your Cub Crews, and hold onto your lion tails as we travel to our Lion Cub Club room.

DAY 1

BIBLE STORY EXPEDITION

TREK TIPS

Preschoolers will enjoy acting out this story, especially if you tell it with enthusiasm and amazement. Be sure to repeat the Bible Point throughout the story to help preschoolers realize that Gideon's faith came from knowing God.

(up to 15 minutes)

Open your Bible to Judges 7:1-22, and show the children the words—it's important for children to understand that the Bible story is true and that it comes from God's Word. Ask the children to sit on the floor while they participate in a Bible story about how Gideon learned to know God. Choose a child to be Gideon. Invite "Gideon" to stand in front of the class.

SAY: God told a man named Gideon to fight against a large army of men who were enemies of God's people. Gideon was afraid when he heard this. Have Gideon act afraid. **He was the youngest son in his family. He didn't know how to fight in an army. But Gideon knew God. He believed that God would help him.**

So Gideon chose an army of one thousand big, strong men to be in his army. Let's pretend we're all in Gideon's army. Have children and crew leaders stand up, and lead them in cheering, "Go, Gideon!" **But God told Gideon to send many of them back home.** Have half of your crew leaders sit down. **Gideon didn't know how they'd fight the enemy, but Gideon did know God.** ("Wow!")

Then God said to Gideon, "There are *still* too many soldiers. Take them down to the water, and I will show you which soldiers to keep with you and which soldiers you must send home." Gideon didn't know how they'd fight the enemy, but Gideon did know God. ("Wow!") **So Gideon took the soldiers down to the water. God said, "Find which soldiers scoop up the water in their hands."** Cup your hands together with palms up, stick out your tongue, and pretend to lap water up into your mouth.

"Those are the ones who will be in your army. If the men kneel down to drink the water right from the stream, send them home." Direct children to pretend they're scooping up water and drinking it out of their hands. Crew leaders will kneel down and pretend they're drinking from a stream.

Gideon did what God said, and there were only three hundred men left to help Gideon fight the huge armies that were his enemies. Gideon didn't know how they'd fight the enemy, but Gideon did know God. ("Wow!")

God told Gideon not to fight with swords and spears and shields. God had a different plan. Each soldier in Gideon's little army would have a trumpet (lead children in blowing a pretend trumpet) **and a light hidden in a jar.** Have children each hold up one finger like a light then cup their other hand over the "light" to hide it.

WHISPER: That night, Gideon's army tiptoed to the enemy's camp. Lead children in sneaking around the room on tiptoe. **When Gideon gave the signal, the soldiers took the covers off their lights** (uncover your "light") **and shouted, "A sword for the Lord and for Gideon!"** Lead children in shouting "A sword for the Lord and for Gideon!" **The enemy soldiers woke up and were so scared that they ran away in fear. Gideon's**

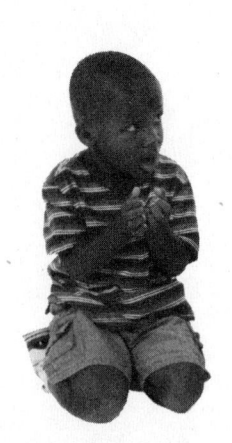

army had won! Lead children in cheering, then have them sit down with their crew leaders. **ASK:**

- **Did you think Gideon could win a battle without a big army? Why or why not?** (Yes, because God said he could; no, because his army was little.)
- **How did Gideon win the battle?** (By doing what God said; he used lights and covers.)

SAY: Gideon knew God. He believed that God would help him. In your Cub Crews, tell your friends one thing you know about God. Allow about two minutes for kids and leaders to share. Then have a few volunteers share their responses.

Encourage children to clap as they cheer for God and say, **I know God.** ("Wow!")

There's a special verse in our Bible, Psalm 135 verse 5, that says, "I know the greatness of the Lord." Let's say that together. Lead children in saying the verse together. **Let's all remember this special Bible verse. That means we'll store it in our brains so we'll remember it for a long time. We're going to help you remember it by singing a song.**

Sing "I Know the Greatness of the Lord" to the tune of "Rejoice in the Lord Always."

I know the greatness of the Lord *(flex muscles),*

Psalm 135 verse 5. *(Clap, clap.)*

I know the greatness of the Lord *(flex muscles),*

Psalm 135 verse 5. *(Clap, clap.)*

I know God. *(Point to temple.)*

I know God.

I know our great big God!

I know God. *(Point to temple.)*

I know God.

I know our great big God!

I know the greatness of the Lord *(flex muscles),*

Psalm 135 verse 5. *(Clap, clap.)*

Now let's get ready for our Cub Club Craft Play, where we'll learn more about how to know God. ("Wow!")

DAY 1

HINTS FROM THE HERD

Our preschool director noted how much kids enjoyed the Treasure Verse songs each day. We hadn't written a song for one of the days, and the preschoolers asked her why they didn't get to sing a Bible verse. What a fun way to hide God's Word in your heart!

DAY 1

CUB CLUB CRAFT PLAY

(up to 20 minutes)

Because the Cub Club Craft Play activities all reinforce the lesson your children learned during the Bible Story Expedition, encourage your Cub Crew Leaders to involve their Cub Crews in as many options as possible.

> Before class each day, set up several or all of the Cub Club Craft Play activities. If you're using the same room for the Bible story and these activities, you may want to cover up the stations with sheets or plastic tablecloths to keep children's attention focused on you until you're ready to begin these activities.
>
> Photocopy and cut out the instructions for each day's Cub Club Craft Play activities. Place a copy of the appropriate instructions near each activity. Cub Crew Leaders can read the instructions and help children complete the activities. (You may want to slip the instructions into plastic sheet protectors to keep them in good condition—especially at the art tables!)
>
> If the children in your class are too young to stay in structured groups for very long, you may want to place one Cub Crew Leader at each station and let children move from station to station individually.

OPTION 1: BIBLE BUDDY DRUMS

1. Use a permanent marker to write each child's name on a Bible Buddy Drum base.

2. Distribute the drum bases, and allow children to decorate them with Serengeti Trek stickers.

3. While children are decorating, work one-on-one with each child. Tie a 12-inch length of yarn around the skinny part of the drum, just below the wide end. (Be sure not to tie this cord too tight since children will "sew" the plastic lacing under it.) Tie a length of plastic lacing to the yarn.

4. Hold the drum cover over the wide end, and help children use the lacing to sew through the holes. When the cover is completely sewn on, tie the end to the yarn.

5. As children work, talk about how people in the Serengeti use drums to talk to each other. Point out that the people listen for drumbeats they know. Talk about how we listen to and obey God because we [] know God.

TREK TIPS

This one-on-one craft is excellent for the first day, allowing Cub Crew Leaders time to talk with each child individually. Be sure to point out that the Bible Buddy Drums will be used to hold some special friends each day.

OPTION 2: GOLDEN HORNS AND GLOWING TORCHES

1. Tear each child's Day 1 Bible Activity page from his or her Cub Club Bible Book. Put each child's name on his or her paper.

2. Direct children to glue Bugles snacks onto the trumpets.

3. Direct children to glue red, orange, and yellow tissue paper onto the torches. Remind children that Gideon knew God and they can [] know God too.

4. After children have finished working on their activity pages, turn them over, and discuss the Daily Challenge with the children. Help each child choose and circle the Challenge he or she will accomplish today.

Permission to photocopy these options from Group's Serengeti Trek: Lion Cub Club Preschool Director Manual granted for local church use. Copyright © Group Publishing, Inc., P.O. Box 481, Loveland, CO 80539. www.groupvbs.com

DAY 1

HINTS FROM THE HERD

We originally planned to use paper towel tubes for this craft, but we weren't able to collect enough for each child. So we grabbed sheets of black construction paper and rolled them into tubes...voilà! These were easier to get than paper towel tubes and worked just as well.

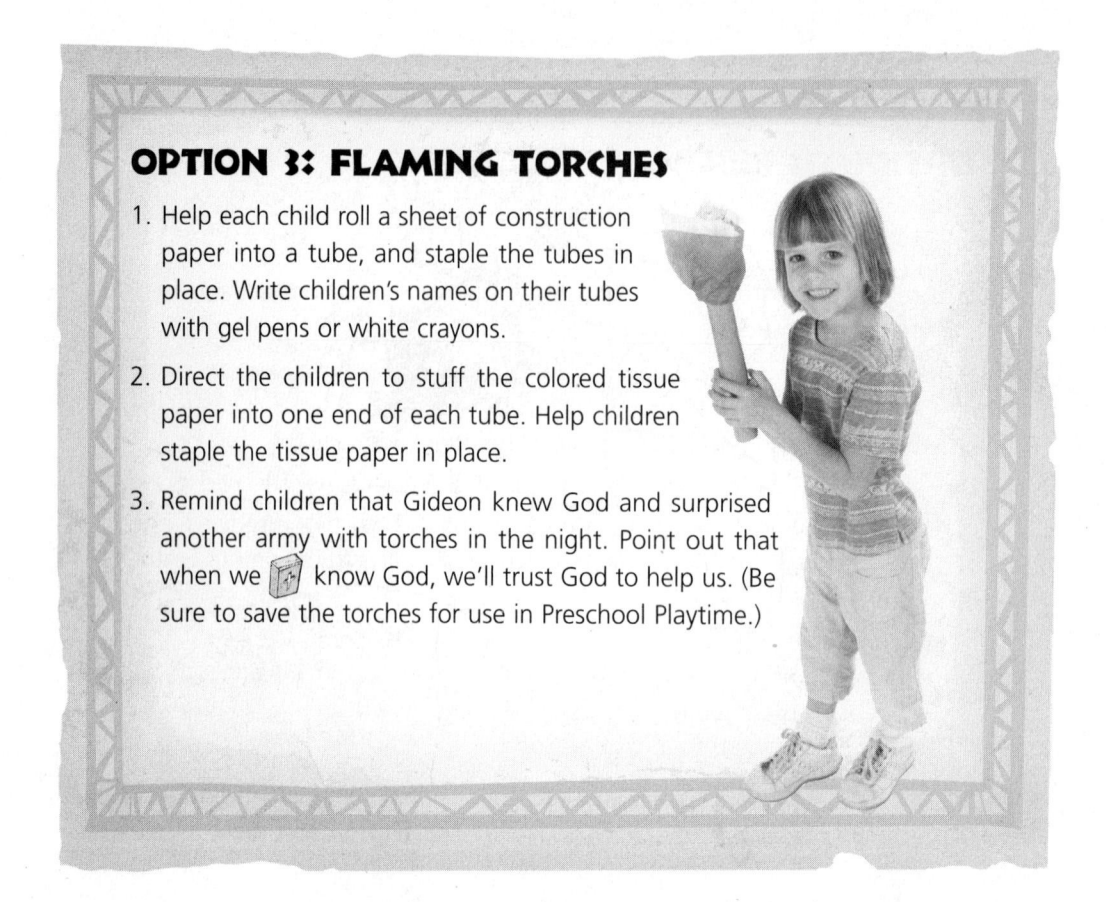

OPTION 3: FLAMING TORCHES

1. Help each child roll a sheet of construction paper into a tube, and staple the tubes in place. Write children's names on their tubes with gel pens or white crayons.

2. Direct the children to stuff the colored tissue paper into one end of each tube. Help children staple the tissue paper in place.

3. Remind children that Gideon knew God and surprised another army with torches in the night. Point out that when we [ ] know God, we'll trust God to help us. (Be sure to save the torches for use in Preschool Playtime.)

OPTION 4: WATER DRINKING

1. Set a large tarp or old shower curtain on the floor. Set some disposable paper bowls of water on the tarp. (Each child should have a different bowl.)

2. Direct the children to re-enact the story they heard about how Gideon chose the men to be in his army. Say: God gave Gideon a big job to do. Gideon had to set up a test to choose the right men for his army. Show the children the two ways Gideon's men drank the water (by lapping it up like a puppy or by scooping it into their hands and drinking it). Say: The men who drank with their hands were the ones Gideon chose for his army.

3. Remind children that Gideon knew God and they can [ ] know God too.

Permission to photocopy these options from Group's Serengeti Trek: Lion Cub Club Preschool Director Manual granted for local church use. Copyright © Group Publishing, Inc., P.O. Box 481, Loveland, CO 80539. www.groupvbs.com

After about seventeen to twenty minutes, shake the tic tac drum, and announce that it's time for the children to clean up the Cub Club Craft Play and get ready to do some other fun activities. When cleanup is complete, use your tic tac drum again, and wait for the children to gather in their Cub Crews.

SAY: Hey, Serengeti Trek friends—now we get to go see a movie! The movie is about a chipmunk named Chadder. Chadder has lots of crazy adventures. I wonder what he'll be doing today!

CHADDER'S ADVENTURE THEATER

(up to 15 minutes)

Lead the children to the place where you've set up a TV and a VCR or DVD player in your classroom. Turn on the video, and watch the Day 1 segment of Chadder's adventure. When the video segment ends, turn off the video.

SAY: I'm glad that Chadder knows God. ("Wow!") It looks like Chadder is going to need God during his Serengeti trek. He's on a special mission to help kids in Africa. Circle up with your Cub Crew so we can talk about this a little more. When I say "circle up," that means to make a little knee-to-knee circle with your crew. Allow kids time to circle up.

SAY: Let everyone in your crew tell about a time they helped someone. I'll give you about two minutes to share. Play "I Want to Know You (In the Secret)" from the *Sing & Play Roar Music* CD. When the song ends, turn off the CD.

SAY: Helping others is one way to show that we know God. ("Wow!") That's because God *helps* us. When we do things God might do, we show that we know God. ("Wow!") **ASK:**

- What else can you do to show that you know God? (Talk about God; pray; tell people about God.)

SAY: Chadder is in for quite an adventure! I hope he watches out for that tricky Dr. Gallstone! I'm glad Chadder has a friend like Jabari—someone he knows! I know God. ("Wow!") **Let's all shout "Wow!" to show that we know God is awesome.** Lead children in shouting "Wow!"

Now let's go enjoy our special Gideon's Trail Mix snacks!

WATERING HOLE SNACKS

(up to 15 minutes)

Have the children sit at tables or in another eating area. Point out to preschoolers that they'll be eating the Gideon's Trail Mix they made for all the children at Watering Hole Snacks. Show kids the snack and **SAY:** These snacks remind us of how Gideon knew God. Let's see how all these snack items remind us of the Bible story about Gideon. Quickly hold up each snack item to remind children of how it ties to the story of Gideon.

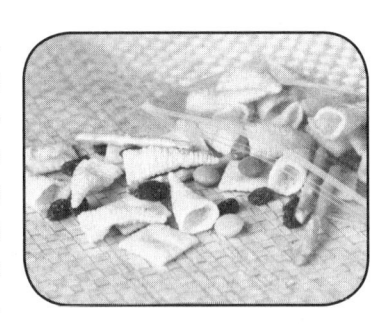

DAY 1

TREK TIPS

As they are cleaning up, have each crew leave together to use the restrooms.

TREK TIPS

You'll be amazed at the difference these knee-to-knee circles can make in your discussions. Crew leaders will have an easier time discussing these important life-application questions. Kids will be more focused, everyone can hear, and crew leaders can easily make eye contact. Insist that kids (and crew leaders) sit in knee-to-knee circles whenever it's time for discussion.

HINTS FROM THE HERD

We were worried when preschoolers had a hard time repeating what they'd seen in the video on the first day. Was it over their heads? Was it too complicated? But on the second day, they warmed up and were excited to see Chadder—and could tell us all about his adventures from the day before. Remember to give preschoolers a little "processing time." After all, Serengeti Trek is a lot of excitement and information in one day!

DAY 1

TREK TIPS

Be sure to remind the children of the wonderful, big job they did by making treats for everyone at Watering Hole Snacks!

HINTS FROM THE HERD

It worked better for us to assign someone to be a leader at each Playtime activity and have that person be the "expert" for all the crews that came to that game. Use your assistant crew leaders, or ask some of your middle school or high school students to come to the preschool area to do this.

Cheese crackers are like the bright torch lights. Bugles remind us of the trumpets they blew. Pretzel sticks are like the swords carried by the Midianites. The few Skittles remind us that there were only a few men in Gideon's army. All the raisins symbolize the countless Midianites.

I know God. ("Wow!") **I know that God loves us and gave us this yummy snack. Let's thank God before we eat.** Lead the children in a simple prayer of thanksgiving. Then give each child a napkin or paper towel, a bag of Gideon's Trail Mix, and a cup half-filled with water. Keep handy a supply of wet wipes for kids to clean their hands and paper towels to wipe up any spills.

As the children eat their snacks, have Cub Crew Leaders talk with the preschoolers to get to know them better. When the children have finished their snacks, have them throw away their cups and other trash. Then shake the tic tac drum, and have the children assemble in their Cub Crews.

PRESCHOOL PLAYTIME

(up to 20 minutes)

If you have the kids go outdoors for playtime, you may want to intersperse unstructured play with some or all of the following activities. If you remain indoors, let the children revisit their favorite Cub Club Craft Play stations, or let them engage in unstructured play. (Some of the following activities may be appropriate for your indoor area. Use your discretion when choosing safe indoor options for Preschool Playtime.)

Photocopy and cut out the instructions for today's Preschool Playtime activities. Place a copy of the appropriate instructions near each station. Cub Crew Leaders can read the instructions and help the children complete the activities.

OPTION 1: GIDEON'S TORCH RELAY

Form two groups, or have two crews visit this station together. Lay your lion tails (10-foot ropes) on the ground, parallel to each other with about five feet between them. Have groups line up behind each lion tail, facing each other. Give the first child in one line a torch made at Cub Club Craft Play. Remind children that Gideon's little army surprised another big army with torches in the night.

Tell the children that the person at the front of the line will carry Gideon's torch to the other team. When the child hands it to the first person in the other line, he or she will say, "Know God!" The recipient will respond by saying "Wow!" and taking the torch. Then that child will carry the torch to the other team, relay-style.

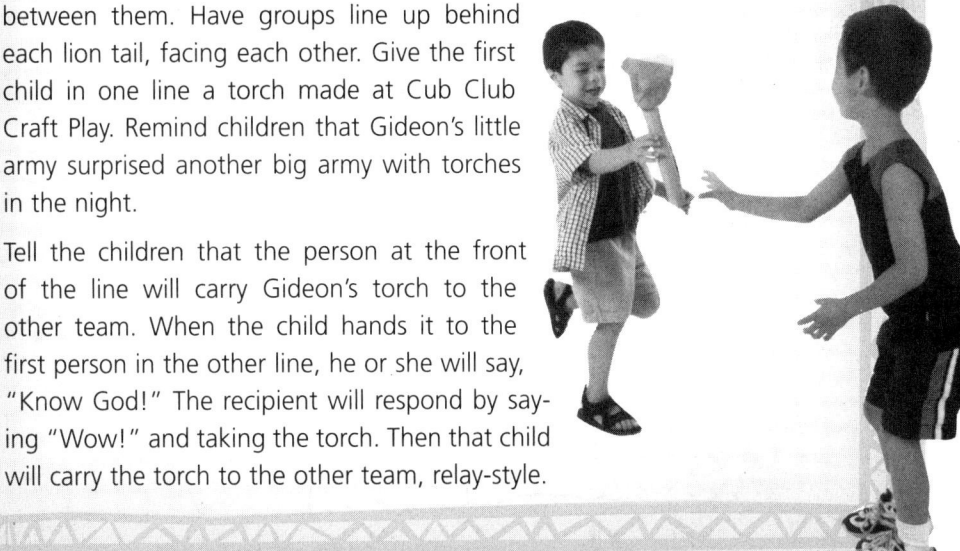

TREK TIPS

This activity uses a paper torch that kids will make during Cub Club Craft Play. If kids haven't made crafts yet, you'll need to make a few torches for this activity. Just roll a sheet of black construction paper into a tube, and staple it in place. Then crumple red, yellow, and orange tissue paper, and stuff it into one end. Staple it in place so the "flames" don't fly out when children run.

OPTION 2: WHO WILL JOIN THE ARMY?

Direct children to hold hands and form a circle. Select one child to be Gideon, and give him or her a toy trumpet or torch (made during Cub Club Craft Play). Remind children that God helped Gideon find people to join his army. Direct the children to march like an army around "Gideon." When the song ends, Gideon will throw the torch in the air. The person who catches it gets to be the next Gideon. While you're marching, sing the following song to the tune of "The Farmer in the Dell."

Gideon knew God.

Gideon knew God.

He fought a mighty enemy,

For Gideon knew God.

Direct the child who catches the torch or trumpet to shout out, "Know God." The rest of the children can respond by saying "Wow!"

Permission to photocopy these options from Group's Serengeti Trek: Lion Cub Club Preschool Director Manual granted for local church use. Copyright © Group Publishing, Inc., P.O. Box 481, Loveland, CO 80539. www.groupvbs.com

DAY 1

TREK TIPS

Since many preschoolers are frightened of being blindfolded, just have children close their eyes. They may peek, but that's OK.

OPTION 3: PIN THE STRIPES ON THE ZEBRA

Before this activity, make a large outline of a zebra on a piece of poster board, using the illustration in the margin. Cut six-inch sections of black crepe-paper streamers, and attach a piece of double-sided tape to the back of each one.

Tell children that zebras know each other by the striped pattern each zebra "wears." Say: Let's see if you can help Zach the Zebra get some stripes.

Have children line up about six feet from the zebra. Let children take turns closing their eyes and trying to tape a stripe onto the zebra. Direct the other children to cheer when preschoolers tape a stripe on Zach.

Point out that zebras know and recognize each other by their special stripes. Explain that we know God because of all the amazing things he does!

OPTION 4: FREE PLAY

If you're outdoors, let the children play with outdoor toys, such as balls, soap bubbles, or sidewalk chalk. Encourage the kids to use sidewalk chalk to draw wild animals on the sidewalk. Children would also enjoy playing on outdoor playground equipment if it's available. If you're indoors, let the children play with classroom toys, such as blocks, stuffed animals, or a water table. As the children play, look for opportunities to review today's Point and Bible story.

Permission to photocopy these options from Group's Serengeti Trek: Lion Cub Club Preschool Director Manual granted for local church use. Copyright © Group Publishing, Inc., P.O. Box 481, Loveland, CO 80539. www.groupvbs.com

After about fifteen minutes, shake the tic tac drum to let the children know it's time to finish their activities and clean up. After cleanup is complete, shake the tic tac drum again. Have the children join their Cub Crews and travel into the classroom for Bible Memory Buddies.

BIBLE MEMORY BUDDIES

DAY 1

(up to 10 minutes)

SAY: I'm going to tell you about someone in our class. Listen to the things I say, and see if you can tell me who I'm thinking of. Choose a crew leader or child, and describe that person without using his or her name. You might say things such as "This friend is wearing a hat" or "I'm thinking of a friend with dark-colored hair worn in a ponytail." Use easy descriptors that will help children guess who you're talking about. After describing a couple of friends, ask:

- **How did you know who I was talking about?** (I looked around the room; you told us what to look for.)

Point to Zach on the Bible Point poster. **SAY: If you were out on the Serengeti, you'd probably see lots of zebras like this. You might think all zebras look alike, with all those crazy stripes! But each zebra has different stripes. Zebras know each other by looking at the special stripes God gave to each one. That's kind of like the way I told you about our friends in class!**

Hold up a Zach the Zebra Bible Memory Buddy. **This friend is named Zach, and he reminds me to 📖 know God.** ("Wow!") **I know that God is awesome because he made all of you wonderful kids! I know that God is powerful because he can make it snow or rain or make it be sunshine. Let's sing our Bible verse song about the greatness of God. This special verse is even written on Zach's tummy!**

Lead kids in singing "I Know the Greatness of the Lord" to the tune of "Rejoice in the Lord Always."

I know the greatness of the Lord *(flex muscles),*

Psalm 135 verse 5. *(Clap, clap.)*

I know the greatness of the Lord *(flex muscles),*

Psalm 135 verse 5. *(Clap, clap.)*

I know God. *(Point to temple.)*

I know God.

I know our great big God!

I know God. *(Point to temple.)*

I know God.

I know our great big God!

I know the greatness of the Lord *(flex muscles),*

Psalm 135 verse 5. *(Clap, clap.)*

Give each crew leader enough Zach Bible Memory Buddies for each child to have one. Instruct crew leaders to hand each child a zebra and say, "[Child's name], you can know the greatness of God!" Crew leaders can help children put their Bible Memory Buddies in their Bible Buddy Drums. On Day 5, children will take home their drums with five Bible Memory Buddies inside.

TREK TIPS

If you aren't using the Bible Point posters as decorations in your room, borrow the Day 1 Bible Point poster from the Sing & Play Roar Leader to use for this activity.

HINTS FROM THE HERD

Don't skip this special one-on-one affirmation time for crews! It's so vital for each child to hear his or her name spoken in a kind and loving way, along with a personal reminder of the Bible verse. These relationship-building times are crucial in helping children build a lasting friendship with Jesus.

DAY 1

TREK TIPS

For safety reasons, it's important that Cub Crew Leaders don't let the children out of their sight until the parents arrive to pick up their children.

SAY: **Now it's time to travel to The Mane Event—a fun time of singing and surprises!** Be sure that children hold hands or hold on to their lion tails as they travel to The Mane Event.

THE MANE EVENT

(up to 20 minutes)

During today's Mane Event, the preschoolers and older kids will sing songs and then watch as a small child demonstrates great "strength" against two older kids. Kids will remember how Gideon's small army defeated the big, mean Midianites.

When the Mane Event Leader dismisses everyone, have the preschoolers remain seated with their Cub Crew Leaders until parents or caregivers arrive to pick up their children. This is a good time for Cub Crew Leaders to collect the children's name badges and put the badges in the Crew Bags.

In some settings, you may want the Mane Event Leader to dismiss the preschoolers first and let parents pick up their children in the Lion Cub Club area.

Remind the children to take home today's activity page from the Cub Club Bible Book, as well as any other projects. Be sure to thank parents and caregivers for bringing their children to Serengeti Trek.

SAFARI SING-ALONG

Preschoolers love to sing, so here are a few songs you can intersperse with your activities. Sing these songs while kids are traveling, playing, waiting in line for the restroom, eating snacks, or when you just happen to have a few extra minutes.

These songs will remind kids to know God.

GIDEON KNEW GOD

(Sing to the tune of "The Farmer in the Dell.")

Gideon knew God.

Gideon knew God.

He fought a mighty enemy,

For Gideon knew God.

I KNOW GOD

(Sing to the tune of "God's Not Dead.")

I know God!

(Shout) **Wow!**

Our God is loving. *(Hug self.)*

I know God!

(Shout) **Wow!**

Our God is loving. *(Hug self.)*

I know God!

(Shout) **Wow!**

Our God is loving. *(Hug self.)*

Yes, I know our loving God.

Repeat this song, substituting other words that describe God, such as *mighty, gentle, awesome,* or *with us.*

DO YOU KNOW?

(Sing to the tune of "Praise Ye the Lord.") You may want to form two groups and have one group sing the "Do you know" line to the other group. The other group will respond with the "Yes, I know God!" line.

Do you know, do you know, do you know, do you know God?

Yes, I know God!

Do you know, do you know, do you know, do you know God?

Yes, I know God!

Yes, I know God!

Do you know him?

Yes, I know God!

Do you know him?

Yes, I know God!

Do you know him?

Yes, I know God!

Permission to photocopy this handout from Group's Serengeti Trek: Lion Cub Club Preschool Director Manual granted for local church use. Copyright © Group Publishing, Inc., P.O. Box 481, Loveland, CO 80539. www.groupvbs.com

LION CUB CLUB
PRESCHOOL DIRECTOR MANUAL

DAY 2

BIBLE POINT:
Talk to God.

BIBLE STORY:
Daniel prays and is sent to the den of lions (Daniel 6:1-28).

TREASURE VERSE:
"Pray at all times" (Ephesians 6:18).

When Nebuchadnezzar conquered Jerusalem, he took many of the young Israelite men into his service. These men—the best and the brightest—would be trained and then be put to use in the king's service. Daniel was one of these young men. During the years of training in Babylon, Daniel lived as a foreigner who was expected to adapt to Babylonian culture, which meant a new name, new foods, and a new religion. But laws and culture couldn't sway Daniel's devotion to God. Faithfully, he prayed. Perhaps Daniel found solace and comfort in his relationship with God. Through prayer, he could stay connected to the God of his people. Even when faced with a den of hungry lions, Daniel refused to stop praying. To Daniel, talking to God was more important than life.

Although society continues to remove prayer from public places, we still have the wonderful freedom to pray. However, the kids at your VBS might still feel a bit like Daniel. They sense the curious stares when they bow their heads to pray in the school cafeteria. They feel like foreigners when they're the only ones not playing a popular video game. That's why prayer is so important in a child's relationship with God. It's a connection to God. It's a reminder of what's really important. It's a place of comfort and acceptance. The activities in today's lesson will help children understand what it means to talk to God.

Because I talk to God, I will

- develop a closer friendship with God,
- feel more comfortable talking *about* God,
- have the comfort of an ever-present friend, and
- make choices that honor and please God.

LION CUB CLUB SCHEDULE

DAY 2

LOCATION	ACTIVITY	MINUTES	WHAT CHILDREN WILL DO	SUPPLIES
Sing & Play Roar	Sing & Play Roar	up to 25	Sing Serengeti Trek songs with the older children.	Name badges, lion tails
Lion Cub Club	Wild Welcome	up to 10	Greet their classmates, and sing a welcoming song.	Name badges, tic tac drum, Bible Story posters
Lion Cub Club	Bible Story Expedition	up to 15	Learn that Daniel talked to God as they listen and do actions to the Bible story.	Bible, "Day 2: Talk About It" questions
Lion Cub Club	Cub Club Craft Play	up to 30	**Option 1: Talk Talk Drums**—Create noisy drums to remind them to talk to God.	Talk Talk Drum Kits, yellow yarn, permanent markers, scissors, tacky glue, paper dessert plates, yellow construction paper, yellow rickrack (optional)
			Option 2: Quiet Lions—Cover the lions' mouths with stickers, and learn about the Daily Challenge.	Cub Club Bible Books, crayons, dot stickers
			Option 3: Lion Masks—Make lion masks to remind them of the lions Daniel faced.	Dinner-size paper plates; brown, orange, and yellow yarn; tacky glue; dessert plates; brown construction paper
			Option 4: Phone a Friend—Pretend to "call" God and talk to him, just as we talk to friends on the phone.	Toy telephones, cell phones, or walkie-talkies
Lion Cub Club	Chadder's Adventure Theater	up to 15	Watch as Chadder Chipmunk learns to talk to God when he encounters difficulties.	TV/VCR or TV/DVD player, *Chadder's Serengeti Trek Adventure* video
Watering Hole Snacks or Lion Cub Club	Watering Hole Snacks	up to 15	Eat Daniel's Lions snacks and learn that Daniel talked to God.	Snacks provided by the Watering Hole Snacks Leader, paper towels, cups of water, wet wipes
Lion Cub Club	Operation Kid-to-Kid	up to 5	Learn about a project in which they'll donate school supplies for needy children.	Operation Kid-to-Kid poster and newsletters, school supply kit
Lion Cub Club or outside	Preschool Playtime	up to 15	**Option 1: Prayer Bridge**—Play a game and pray for each other.	
			Option 2: Daniel, the Lions Are Coming—Use lion masks to sneak up on Daniel while he's praying.	Lion masks made during Cub Club Craft Play
			Option 3: Roll a Prayer—Roll a cube that gives prayer ideas.	Small square box, craft paper, pen
			Option 4: Free Play—Enjoy free play outdoors or in the classroom.	Playground equipment, various outdoor toys, classroom toys
Lion Cub Club	Bible Memory Buddies	up to 10	Roar like lions, and receive a Bible Memory Buddy named Roary the Lion.	Roary Bible Memory Buddies
The Mane Event	The Mane Event	up to 20	Sing songs, and watch a fun game show to learn more about Daniel.	Supplies provided by the Mane Event Leader

LION CUB CLUB PREPARATIONS

DAY 2

Before the children arrive:

- Photocopy the "Day 2: Talk About It" questions on page 55. You'll need one set for each crew. Having the questions on a slip of paper allows crew leaders to guide the discussion in a more personal way.

- Choose the Cub Club Craft Play activities you'll use, photocopy the instructions, and collect and prepare the supplies. Set up each station as shown, and cover the supplies with a sheet.

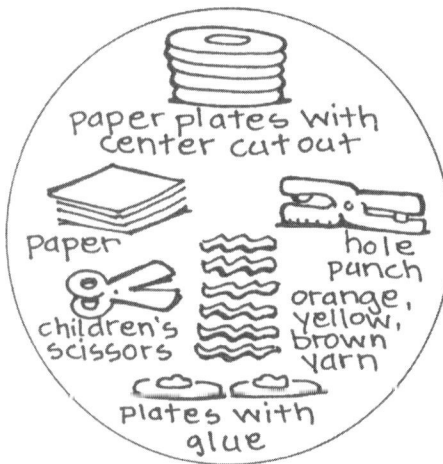

Talk Talk Drums — yellow construction paper triangles, plates with glue on them, short pieces of yellow yarn, Talk Talk Drum Kits, permanent marker

Quiet Lions — dot stickers, crayons

Lion Masks — paper plates with center cut out, paper, children's scissors, hole punch, orange, yellow, brown yarn, plates with glue

Phone a Friend — toy phones & cell phones

- Choose the Preschool Playtime activities you'll use, photocopy the instructions, collect the supplies you'll need, and set out the supplies next to the play areas.

    For the "Roll a Prayer" activity, wrap a small square box in craft paper. On each of the six sides, draw one of the following: two friends, a family, a child, a dog or cat, your church building, and a Cub Crew. (Use the sketches on page 61 as a guideline.)

- Hang up the Day 2 Bible Story poster on a wall near your Bible Story Expedition area.

- Check with the Watering Hole Snacks Leader to find out what time the Watering Hole Snacks Service Crew will deliver your snacks.

DAY 2

TREK TIPS

Take extra measures to let crew leaders, children, and parents know to take children to Sing & Play Roar. (A sign on the door is an easy way to help clear up confusion.)

- Hang up today's Operation Kid-to-Kid poster in your Bible Story Expedition area. Today children will meet Semira.
- Post a sign on your door letting parents know that children will meet their crew leaders at Sing & Play Roar.

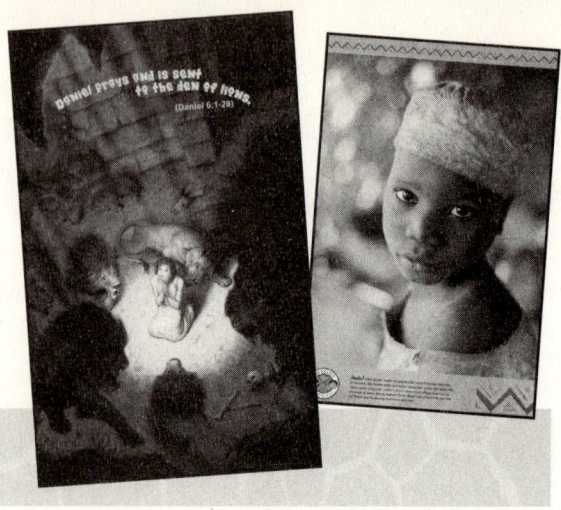

SING & PLAY ROAR

(up to 25 minutes)

Before the children arrive, arrange with the Sing & Play Roar Leader to reserve seats up front for your preschoolers. Plan to have a specific area for each Cub Crew. That way, if some kids arrive late, they'll know where to look for their crews.

Greet the children as they arrive, and have the Cub Crew Leaders give the children their name badges. The crew leaders can sit with children and involve them in this worship time. Preschoolers will enjoy hearing the music and doing the motions with the big kids!

DAILY CHALLENGE

During Sing & Play Roar, kids will have a chance to talk with their Cub Crew Leaders about how they completed the Daily Challenge. Look for ways preschoolers are living out the Bible Point each day during Serengeti Trek. Help them discover the joy of getting wild about God!

After the kids have been dismissed, tell the children to hold on to their lion tails with their Cub Crews and go to the Lion Cub Club room.

WILD WELCOME

(up to 10 minutes)

When the children arrive in your room, make sure each child is wearing his or her name badge. You can expect new children to visit Lion Cub Club each day, so have extra name badges on hand. Assign new children to Cub Crews that have fewer than five children in them. If most of your crews are full, check with the Serengeti Trek Director to see if he or she has recruited extra volunteers who might be available as Cub Crew Leaders.

Shake the tic tac drum to gain children's attention. Introduce yourself, and **SAY: Welcome to Lion Cub Club! Remember my tic tac drum? When I shake my tic tac drum, it means I want you to find your Cub Crews, sit together, and quietly look at me.**

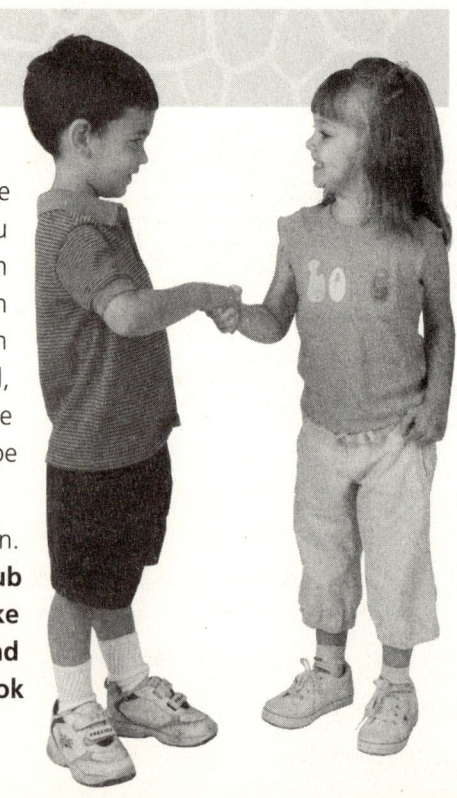

Shake your tic tac drum again. If most of the children were in Lion Cub Club yesterday, they'll probably remember what to do and may even assemble in their Cub Crews without further instructions.

SAY: You did a great job finding your Cub Crews. It's so good to see all your smiling faces here at Lion Cub Club! Let's welcome each other while we sing!

Have the children sing the welcoming song "I'm So Glad" to the tune of "Ten Little Indians." Lead the children in greeting their friends and doing the motions.

I'm so glad my friends are here. *(Shake hands with a friend.)*

I'm so glad my friends are here. *(Shake hands with a friend.)*

I'm so glad my friends are here *(shake hands with a friend)*

At Ser-en-ge-ti Trek!

Roar!

I'm so glad my friends are here. *(Shake hands with a friend.)*

I'm so glad my friends are here. *(Shake hands with a friend.)*

I'm so glad my friends are here *(shake hands with a friend)*

At Ser-en-ge-ti Trek!

Roar!

Point to the Day 1 Bible Story poster, and **SAY: Remember what we learned yesterday when we read the story of Gideon? We discovered that Gideon knew and trusted God. I know God too.** ("Wow!")

Point to the Day 2 Bible Story poster. **Today we're going to learn a Bible story about when Daniel talked to God. Daniel prayed three times every day. We'll learn that we can talk to God too!** ("Wow!") **Let's get ready to hear how Daniel talked to God.**

BIBLE STORY EXPEDITION

(up to 15 minutes)

Have children gather together closely. Open a Bible to the book of Daniel, and show the Bible to the children.

SAY: Our story comes from the Bible, which is God's special book. God wants us to learn from people who lived a long time ago and followed God. Daniel was a man who talked to God. ("Wow!")

While I tell you this Bible story, I'm going to need your help.

Choose "hammy" crew leaders to be Daniel and Darius. Ask three children to be the "bad guys," and explain that the rest of the children will be the lions. Explain that your actors need to listen and have fun acting out their roles.

DAY 2

HINTS FROM THE HERD

Teenagers and adults had fun hamming it up in their roles, making this drama more exciting. And little ones loved being the fierce—but silent—lions!

Darius was a king who lived long ago.
The king had lots of power, you know! *(Darius flexes muscles.)*
He picked out three men who would help him the most. *(Point to the "bad guys.")*
Daniel was named to the number one post. *(Point to Daniel.)*

Daniel was glad to advise the king.
With wisdom from God, he could solve anything.
So near his window each morning and night *(Daniel kneels to pray),*
Daniel prayed and asked God to help him do right.

The king's other helpers were greedy, mean fellas. *(Bad guys rub hands together.)*
Having Daniel in charge sure made them all jealous.
They waited and watched for Daniel to do something wrong.
Never has anyone waited so long!

They stormed and they stewed and they thought night and day. *(Bad guys scratch chins.)*
They'd get Daniel in trouble—there must be a way!
They thought and they thought, then one said with a nod,
"Let's get Daniel in trouble for praying to God!"

We'll make a new law! Here's what it will say:
People must pray to the *king* when they pray. *(Everyone points to Darius.)*
We'll get the king to sign with the seal of his ring.
Not a word can be changed. Not a bit! Not a thing!

As soon as King Darius signed the new law,
They went after Daniel, and here's what they saw:
Daniel was in his house, down on his knees *(Daniel kneels to pray),*
Praying to God just as bold as you please!

They dragged faithful Daniel off to the king *(bad guys pull Daniel to Darius)*
And said, "He's been doing a terrible thing *(bad guys point to Daniel)*—
Praying to God! Now don't you forget—
The law says he must be thrown into the lions' pit."

There was no way that Darius could save his adviser. *(Darius looks sad.)*
He said sadly, "Daniel, I should have been wiser!
I shouldn't have listened to these evil men.
May your God protect you in that lions' den!"

The king woke the next morning and jumped out of bed. *(Darius yawns, stretches, and jumps up.)*
He threw his robe 'round his shoulders, his crown on his head.
He threw open the doors and flew from his room.
He had to find out what happened to Daniel, and soon.

As fast as he could, the king ran to the den *(Darius runs around room and back to Daniel),*
Sure that the lions had eaten his friend.
He stopped, looked, and listened but heard not a sound.
Those cats were the quietest lions around!

"Daniel!" he called. *(Darius cups hands to mouth.)* **"Did the God you love a bunch
Keep you from being the lions' lunch?"**
"Yes!" Daniel answered. "I talked to God through the night,
And an angel shut all the lions' mouths tight!

"The great God I worship would never desert me. *(Daniel points up.)*
Not once did those big hungry cats try to hurt me.
Not a growl did I hear, not a purr, not a roar,
Not a peep, not a sneeze, not a sniff, not a snore."

The king was delighted, and he gave a great shout,
"Come here, all you servants, and pull Daniel out!" *(Darius pulls Daniel up.)*
To all the bad guys, he said, "This is it.
Now it's your turn to go into the pit!"

Darius made up a new law right away.
"Respect Daniel's God—he saved Daniel today!"
Then to the whole kingdom, they told Daniel's story,
Worshipped the true God, and gave him great glory!

SAY: Daniel talked to God and got in trouble with the king. But when Daniel was in the lions' den, he talked to God and was protected from the lions. When you're in trouble, you can talk to God too. ("Wow!")

Have each Cub Crew sit in a tight, knee-to-knee circle. Distribute the "Day 2: Talk About It" questions. Allow about three minutes for crews to discuss the questions.

DAY 2: TALK ABOUT IT

- **What happened to Daniel?** (He prayed; he was thrown into a lions' den; God saved Daniel from the lions.)
- **How do you think Daniel felt when God answered his prayers?** (He thanked God; he was happy.)
- **What can you talk to God about?** (My grandma who is sick; my friends.)

Permission to photocopy these questions from Group's Serengeti Trek: Lion Cub Club Preschool Director Manual granted for local church use. Copyright © Group Publishing, Inc., P.O. Box 481, Loveland, CO 80539. www.groupvbs.com

SAY: You and I can talk to God ("Wow!") just as Daniel did. Let's talk to God right now! ("Wow!")

PRAY: Dear God, thank you for listening to us and letting us talk to you anytime we want to. We love you. Help us serve and follow you as Daniel did. In Jesus' name, amen.

DAY 2

TREK TIPS

Many people question whether preschool children can participate in discussions. We found that preschool kids love to talk when someone is interested in what they have to say. Encourage your crew leaders to prompt them and give them eye-to-eye contact.

DAY 2

Lead children in the following song to the tune of "Sailing, Sailing."

Daniel, Daniel,

Daniel talked to God.

When he was afraid, he prayed.

Yes, Daniel talked to God.

Talking, praying,

I can talk to God.

Whenever I'm afraid, I'll pray.

I can talk to God.

SAY: It's time to have some fun at our Cub Club Craft Play. Your Cub Crew Leader will help you at each station.

CUB CLUB CRAFT PLAY

(up to 30 minutes)

TREK TIPS

You may want to use Glue Dots to hold the lion ears in place. Glue Dots are available at www.groupoutlet.com.

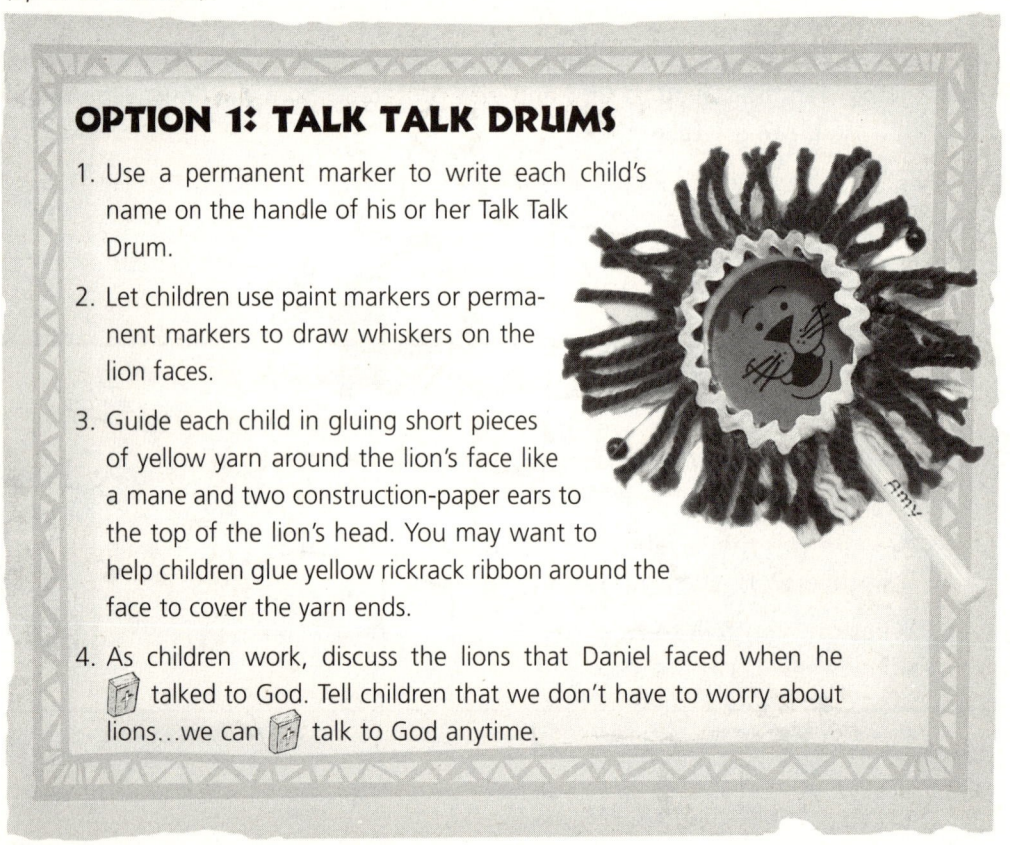

OPTION 1: TALK TALK DRUMS

1. Use a permanent marker to write each child's name on the handle of his or her Talk Talk Drum.

2. Let children use paint markers or permanent markers to draw whiskers on the lion faces.

3. Guide each child in gluing short pieces of yellow yarn around the lion's face like a mane and two construction-paper ears to the top of the lion's head. You may want to help children glue yellow rickrack ribbon around the face to cover the yarn ends.

4. As children work, discuss the lions that Daniel faced when he talked to God. Tell children that we don't have to worry about lions…we can talk to God anytime.

Permission to photocopy these options from Group's Serengeti Trek: Lion Cub Club Preschool Director Manual granted for local church use. Copyright © Group Publishing, Inc., P.O. Box 481, Loveland, CO 80539. www.groupvbs.com

OPTION 2: QUIET LIONS

1. Give each child the Day 2 Bible Activity page from his or her Cub Club Bible Book, and write the child's name on his or her paper.

2. Direct children to place a dot sticker over each lion's mouth to show that God heard Daniel's prayer and shut the lions' mouths. Children may color the picture of Daniel praying in the den of lions.

3. Remind children that they can 📖 talk to God just as Daniel did.

4. Turn the children's Bible Activity pages over, and discuss the Daily Challenge with them. Let each child choose and circle which Challenge he or she will accomplish.

OPTION 3: LION MASKS

1. Set out paper plates with the center circle cut out. Write each child's name on the back of his or her plate.

2. Direct children to glue pieces of yellow, brown, and orange yarn around each circle to make a lion's mane. Help children cut out triangular ears from construction paper and glue them to the top of the paper plates.

3. Remind children of what happened to Daniel and how God protected him when he was in the lions' den. Talk about times we can 📖 talk to God.

4. Encourage children to hold the masks up to their faces and to say, "I 📖 talk to God." (Save the lion masks to use at Preschool Playtime.)

OPTION 4: PHONE A FRIEND

1. Set out a variety of toy telephones, cell phones, or walkie-talkies.

2. Let children pretend to talk to friends on the phone.

3. Point out that Daniel talked to God all the time because he loved God like a good friend. Encourage children to pretend they're talking to God on the toy phones. Remind them that they can 📖 talk to God about anything.

Permission to photocopy these options from Group's Serengeti Trek: Lion Cub Club Preschool Director Manual granted for local church use. Copyright © Group Publishing, Inc., P.O. Box 481, Loveland, CO 80539. www.groupvbs.com

DAY 2

HINTS FROM THE HERD

We realized that it helped to summarize what had happened in Chadder since we had new children coming every day. Plus, it reminded kids where the action had left off the day before.

After about seventeen to twenty minutes, shake the tic tac drum, and announce that it's time for the children to clean up Cub Club Craft Play and get ready to do some other fun activities. When cleanup is complete, use your tic tac drum again, and wait for the children to gather in their Cub Crews.

SAY: Now we're going to go back to our story area to see a video! Do you remember our new friend, Chadder Chipmunk? We met him yesterday. **ASK:**

- **What do you remember about Chadder's adventure?** (Chadder was on a mission; he was in Africa; there was a bad guy.)

SAY: Chadder is on a mission to help children in Africa. He's bringing some important medicine so the children can get well. But sneaky Dr. Gallstone is mad that Chadder didn't ride with him. Dr. Gallstone wants to be famous for delivering the medicine. Let's see if Dr. Gallstone gives Chadder and his friend Jabari any trouble today.

CHADDER'S ADVENTURE THEATER

(up to 15 minutes)

Lead the children to the place where you've set up a TV and a VCR or DVD player in your classroom, and let the children watch today's portion of the *Chadder's Serengeti Trek Adventure* video.

When the video segment ends, **SAY:** Chadder sure learned a lot about talking to God! **ASK:**

- **Why did Chadder want to talk to God?** (He was scared of the lions; he was afraid.)
- **Who is helping Chadder?** (Jabari; Auntie Juji; his teddy bear.)
- **If you were on the Serengeti Trek, how would you help Chadder do the right thing?** (I'd be his friend; I'd help him talk to God; I'd give him a hug.)

SAY: When Chadder was afraid of the lions, he talked to God. I [📖] talk to God too. ("Wow!") When I'm afraid or sad or happy, I'm glad I can [📖] talk to God! ("Wow!")

WATERING HOLE SNACKS

(up to 15 minutes)

Have the children sit at tables or in another eating area. Point out that today's snack reminds us of what happened when Daniel [📖] talked to God. ("Wow!") Show children that the lions don't have mouths because God shut the lions' mouths. Lead the children in a simple prayer of thanksgiving. Then give each child a napkin or paper towel, a Daniel's Lions snack, and a cup half-filled with water. Keep handy a supply of wet wipes for kids to clean their hands and paper towels to wipe up any spills. When the children have finished their snacks, have them throw away their cups and other trash. Shake the tic tac drum, and lead children to your Bible story area.

OPERATION KID-TO-KID™

(up to 5 minutes)

Have the Cub Crews gather near the Operation Kid-to-Kid poster.
ASK:

- **How many of you go to preschool?**
- **What do you learn at preschool?** (My numbers; how to play with my friends; songs.)
- **What other fun things do you like to do at preschool?** (Play on the playground; make crafts; go on field trips.)

SAY: **Here in [name of your community], we have plenty of paper, pencils, crayons, glue, and scissors. But imagine going to a preschool where there weren't any of those things. You couldn't draw or do fun art projects. You couldn't learn to write your name. That would make me feel sad!**

Point to the poster and **SAY:** **This is Semira. Kids like Semira want to go to school so they can learn. But they don't have any pencils or paper or crayons. That makes them feel sad because they really want to learn. But you and I can help! This week we'll collect special things to help kids like Semira in school.** Hold up a completed school-supply kit. **We'll put the supplies in special bags to make school kits.**

Hold up the Operation Kid-to-Kid newsletter. **SAY:** **Your Cub Crew Leaders will have a paper just like this for each person. It shows all the things we need to collect. In your crews, decide who will bring which item—some people may have to bring two things. Then your crew leader will circle the school supplies you need to bring.**

Distribute the Operation Kid-to-Kid newsletters. Allow crews a minute or two to work together and decide who will bring each item. Have Cub Crew Leaders circle the item or items on each child's handout. Let crew leaders place the completed handouts in the Crew Bag and prepare kids for Preschool Playtime.

If you'll be going outdoors for Preschool Playtime, have the children hold on to their lion tails and follow their crew leaders outside.

PRESCHOOL PLAYTIME

(up to 15 minutes)

Take children outdoors, have them visit their favorite Cub Club Craft Play stations again, or let them engage in unstructured play. If you choose to go outdoors, intersperse some of the following activities with unstructured play.

DAY 2

TREK TIPS

During today's Mane Event, elementary kids will hear about Operation Kid-to-Kid for the first time. They'll also gather with their crews to talk about which items they'll bring. Use this time at The Mane Event for crew leaders to remind preschoolers about which school supplies to bring. The extra reinforcement will really bring this mission project home!

DAY 2

HINTS FROM THE HERD

Although most kids were too shy to pray aloud, they were happy to bow their heads and pray while the leader said a short prayer about the thing the child had named. Use this as a time to model an attitude of enthusiasm and excitement about prayer.

OPTION 1: PRAYER BRIDGE

Help children form a line. Choose a child to join hands with you, forming a "bridge."

SAY: In today's Bible story, Daniel talked to God. We can 📖 talk to God too. ("Wow!") **I want you to think of something we can pray for as you begin to march under the bridge.** Encourage the line of children to march under the bridge.

Sing this song to the tune of "London Bridge."

God will listen when you pray,

When you pray, when you pray.

God will listen when you pray.

Talk to God!

Drop the bridge around a child. Ask the child to name something or someone you can pray about together. Say a sentence prayer with the child, then raise the bridge and start the song over again. Continue until everyone in your crew has had a chance to be captured and pray.

HINTS FROM THE HERD

Since some kids hadn't made their lion masks, our games leader grabbed a few plates with the centers cut out and simply wrapped a long length of yarn around each one—almost like making a wreath. It was a quick way to make the lion masks without using glue.

OPTION 2: DANIEL, THE LIONS ARE COMING

Gather your Cub Crew together, and hand out the lion masks they made during Cub Club Craft Play.

Choose one child to be "Daniel." (Daniel won't need a lion mask.) Have Daniel stand on the far side of the area with his or her back turned to the rest of the group. Guide the other children in pretending to be lions, holding their masks to their faces. The lions will quietly creep up and try to touch Daniel before Daniel hears them. If Daniel hears a noise, he or she will quickly turn around and yell "I 📖 talk to God!" The lions must freeze in place while Daniel guesses who made the sound. If Daniel guesses correctly, that lion must go back to the starting place. Then have Daniel turn his back to the lions again. The first lion to touch Daniel gets a big hug from that child and becomes the next Daniel.

Permission to photocopy these options from Group's Serengeti Trek: Lion Cub Club Preschool Director Manual granted for local church use. Copyright © Group Publishing, Inc., P.O. Box 481, Loveland, CO 80539. www.groupvbs.com

DAY 2

OPTION 3: ROLL A PRAYER

Form a circle, and let children sit down. Remind children that Daniel prayed all the time about everything. Explain that you'll use the cube to help kids pray for lots of different things. Show children the cube, and explain what each picture represents. Let children take turns rolling the cube, then lead them in a sentence prayer for the subject that is showing on the cube.

You | Friends | Your Family | Pets | Our Church | Our Cub Crew

HINTS FROM THE HERD

This was a favorite game! Children really got into praying for a variety of things, and leaders were touched at what kids prayed for. When one little girl rolled the "friends" picture, she prayed for her sister, thanking God for "the best sister ever." Wow!

OPTION 4: FREE PLAY

If you're outdoors, let the children play with outdoor toys, such as balls, soap bubbles, or sidewalk chalk. Children would also enjoy playing on outdoor playground equipment if it's available. If you're indoors, let the children play with classroom toys, such as blocks, stuffed animals, or a water table. As the children play, look for opportunities to review today's Point and Bible story.

Permission to photocopy these options from Group's Serengeti Trek: Lion Cub Club Preschool Director Manual granted for local church use. Copyright © Group Publishing, Inc., P.O. Box 481, Loveland, CO 80539. www.groupvbs.com

After ten to fifteen minutes, shake your tic tac drum to let the children know it's time to finish their activities and clean up. After cleanup is complete, use the tic tac drum again. Have the children join their Cub Crews and gather in the Bible story area for Bible Memory Buddies.

DAY 2

BIBLE MEMORY BUDDIES

(up to 10 minutes)

Hold up a Roary the Lion Bible Memory Buddy. Let children give you their biggest lion's roar.

SAY: Wow, you're sure a bunch of noisy lions! All that roaring reminds me that we can make noise when we talk to God. ("Wow!") **My friend Roary here likes to make a lovely noise when he talks to God. He even has a special Bible verse written on him.** Read Ephesians 6:18 from Roary's belly: "Pray at all times." Lead children in the following song to the tune of "Clementine."

Pray at all times.

Pray at all times.

God is always listening.

Pray at all times.

Pray at all times,

Says Ephesians 6:18.

Let children offer examples of times they can pray, such as at breakfast, when they're swinging, or at bedtime. Have children act out what they do during those times as they sing. For example, children might lay their heads on their hands to pretend they're falling asleep.

SAY: God is always listening when we talk to him. Crew leaders, as you give each child a Roary Bible Memory Buddy, remind that child to talk to God at all times. Say, "[Child's name]**, you can talk to God."**

Distribute Bible Memory Buddies to crew leaders, then allow crews to circle up for this special affirmation time.

Have the Cub Crew Leaders collect the children's crafts from Cub Club Craft Play to take to The Mane Event. Shake your tic tac drum, and have the children assemble in their Cub Crews, holding on to their lion tails.

THE MANE EVENT

(up to 20 minutes)

Lead the children to The Mane Event. There, preschoolers will sing with the older kids and participate in a fun game show about Daniel.

When the Mane Event Leader dismisses everyone, have the preschoolers remain seated with their Cub Crew Leaders until parents or caregivers arrive to pick up their children. This is a good time for crew leaders to collect the children's name badges and put them in the Crew Bags. In some settings, you may want the Mane Event Leader to dismiss the preschoolers first and let parents pick up their children in the Lion Cub Club area.

Remind the children to take today's Bible Activity page and other projects with them when they leave. Be sure to thank parents and caregivers for bringing their children to Serengeti Trek.

HINTS FROM THE HERD

To make sure our preschoolers were connecting with their parents, we preferred returning to the preschool area to release children to their parents.

SAFARI SING-ALONG

Preschoolers love to sing, so here are a few songs you can intersperse with your activities. Sing these songs while kids are traveling, playing, waiting in line for the restroom, eating snacks, or when you just happen to have a few extra minutes.

These songs will remind kids to 📖 talk to God.

THIS IS THE WAY

(Direct children to get in a circle and hold hands. Sing the following song to the tune of "The Mulberry Bush." Have children take turns naming when, where, or how they can talk to God. Here are some examples: play dolls, ride in the car, go to bed, or pick up toys. Have the children act out the suggestions as they sing the verse again.)

This is the way we talk to God, talk to God, talk to God.

This is the way we talk to God

When we...

PRAY AT ALL TIMES

(Sing to the tune of "Clementine.")

Pray at all times.

Pray at all times.

God is always listening.

Pray at all times.

Pray at all times,

Says Ephesians 6:18.

DANIEL, DANIEL

(Sing to the tune of "Sailing, Sailing.")

Daniel, Daniel,

Daniel talked to God.

When he was afraid, he prayed.

Yes, Daniel talked to God.

Talking, praying,

I can talk to God.

Whenever I'm afraid, I'll pray.

I can talk to God.

Permission to photocopy this handout from Group's Serengeti Trek: Lion Cub Club Preschool Director Manual granted for local church use. Copyright © Group Publishing, Inc., P.O. Box 481, Loveland, CO 80539. www.groupvbs.com

LION CUB CLUB
PRESCHOOL DIRECTOR MANUAL
DAY 3

BIBLE POINT:
Tell about God.

BIBLE STORY:
Shadrach, Meshach, and Abednego stand up for God (Daniel 3:1-30).

TREASURE VERSE:
"I will tell of all the marvelous things you have done" (Psalm 9:1b).

When King Nebuchadnezzar captured Jerusalem, Daniel's friends Shadrach, Meshach, and Abednego were also taken to Babylon. In Babylon, the three friends served under the most powerful ruler of the time. Nebuchadnezzar considered himself the supreme political and spiritual authority. Dissenting viewpoints or actions were unacceptable and intolerable. So when Shadrach, Meshach, and Abednego refused to bow to Nebuchadnezzar's golden image, the enraged king commanded their gruesome death. The young men didn't know that God would save them. They went to the furnace with the realization that this could be a funeral pyre. Yet amazingly, the three friends stood firm in their love for and belief in the one true God. They boldly proclaimed God's faithfulness. Even when the heat was on, Shadrach, Meshach, and Abednego wouldn't stop talking about God.

Kids today are encouraged to "bow" to many things, from celebrities to bad language. And it's far too easy to fall into bad habits when it seems as if "everyone else is doing it." While younger children are bold in their faith, older kids might feel strange talking about their relationship with God. That's why it's crucial to instill a courageous faith in the hearts of kids today. Help kids discover that they *can* stand up for God—even by simply telling others about him, talking about him, or speaking his name proudly and with reverence. The activities in today's lesson will guide kids as they explore what it means to tell about God.

Because I tell about God, I will

- be bold in sharing my faith,
- let others know more about God,
- show others what it means to be God's friend, and
- help others be bold in their faith.

LION CUB CLUB SCHEDULE

DAY 3

LOCATION	ACTIVITY	MINUTES	WHAT CHILDREN WILL DO	SUPPLIES
Sing & Play Roar	Sing & Play Roar	up to 25	Sing Serengeti Trek songs with the older children.	Name badges, lion tails
Lion Cub Club	Wild Welcome	up to 10	Greet their classmates, and sing a welcoming song.	Name badges, tic tac drum, Bible Story posters
Lion Cub Club	Bible Story Expedition	up to 15	Use blocks to build part of the story of Shadrach, Meshach, and Abednego.	Bible; blocks; red, yellow, and orange tissue paper; craft sticks; "Day 3: Talk About It" questions
Lion Cub Club	Cub Club Craft Play	up to 30	**Option 1: Wildlife Photo Frames**—Create colorful photo frames to celebrate some of the great things God has made.	African animal picture books, Wildlife Photo Frame Kits, Glue Dots
			Option 2: Appearing Angel—Draw an angel next to the men in the furnace, color in the flames, and discuss the Daily Challenge.	Cub Club Bible Books, watercolor paints, paintbrushes, water, white crayons
			Option 3: Talk-a-Phone—Make megaphones to tell about God.	White paper plates, Serengeti Trek stickers, colored markers, stapler, scissors
			Option 4: On Fire for God—Use blocks and paper to act out the Bible story.	Blocks; red, orange, and yellow tissue paper
Lion Cub Club	Chadder's Adventure Theater	up to 15	See if Chadder and Jabari can outwit Dr. Gallstone.	TV/VCR or TV/DVD player, *Chadder's Serengeti Trek Adventure* video
Watering Hole Snacks or Lion Cub Club	Watering Hole Snacks	up to 15	Eat Meshach snacks prepared by older kids.	Snacks provided by the Watering Hole Snacks Leader, paper towels, cups of water, wet wipes
Lion Cub Club	Operation Kid-to-Kid	up to 5	Cheer for friends who brought in new school supply items.	Operation Kid-to-Kid poster
Lion Cub Club or outside	Preschool Playtime	up to 15	**Option 1: Four in the Fire**—Play a game to remind them of the fourth helper in the furnace.	Red and orange crepe-paper streamers
			Option 2: Talk-a-Thon—Use megaphones to repeat the Bible verse.	Megaphones made in Cub Club Craft Play
			Option 3: Pass the Word—Pass a message and practice telling about God.	
			Option 4: Free Play—Enjoy free play outdoors or in the classroom.	Playground equipment, various outdoor toys, classroom toys
Lion Cub Club	Bible Memory Buddies	up to 10	Chatter like cranes, then receive a Bible Memory Buddy named Elaine the Crane.	Elaine the Crane Bible Memory Buddies
The Mane Event	The Mane Event	up to 20	Sing songs, and create a fiery furnace!	Supplies provided by the Mane Event Leader

LION CUB CLUB PREPARATIONS

DAY 3

Before the children arrive:

- For Bible Story Expedition, gather a set of the following materials for each Cub Crew: ten blocks; red, orange, and yellow tissue paper; and four wide craft sticks. Photocopy the "Day 3: Talk About It" questions on page 71. You'll need one set of questions for each crew.

- Choose the Cub Club Craft Play activities you'll use, photocopy the instructions, and collect and prepare the supplies. Set up each station as shown, and cover the supplies with a sheet.

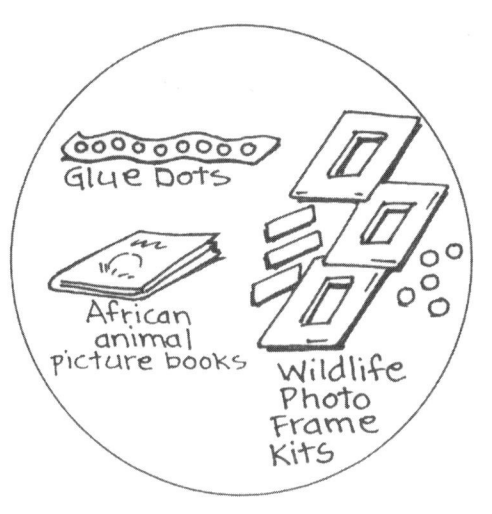

> **HINTS FROM THE HERD**
>
> At our local library, we found books filled with gorgeous photos of animals of the Serengeti. Showing children these pictures will really help connect the "Wildlife Photo Frames" craft with the Bible Point. (Plus, the photos are simply amazing to look at!)

Wildlife Photo Frames
- Glue Dots
- African animal picture books
- Wildlife Photo Frame Kits

Appearing Angel
- white crayons
- cups of water
- watercolor paints and paintbrushes

Talk-a-Phone
- paper plates
- Serengeti Trek stickers
- scissors
- markers
- stapler

On Fire for God
- blocks
- craft sticks
- red, orange, and yellow tissue paper

- Choose the Preschool Playtime activities you'll use, photocopy the instructions, collect the supplies you'll need, and set out the supplies next to the play areas.

- Hang up the Day 3 Bible Story poster on a wall near your Bible Story Expedition area.

DAY 3

- Check with the Watering Hole Snacks Leader to find out what time the Service Crew will deliver your snacks or when they want you to come to Watering Hole Snacks.
- Hang up today's Operation Kid-to-Kid poster in your Bible Story Expedition area. Today children will meet Ajani.
- Post a sign on your door letting parents know that children will meet their crew leaders at Sing & Play Roar.

SING & PLAY ROAR

(up to 25 minutes)

Before the children arrive, arrange with the Sing & Play Roar Leader to reserve seats up front for your preschoolers. Plan to have a specific area for each Cub Crew. That way, if some kids arrive late, they'll know where to look for their crews.

Greet the children as they arrive, and have the Cub Crew Leaders give the children their name badges. Have Cub Crew Leaders collect any school supplies children have brought and place them in their Crew Bags. (They can drop off the supplies in your designated Operation Kid-to-Kid area when they return to the Lion Cub Club classroom.) The crew leaders can sit with children and involve them in this worship time. Preschoolers will enjoy hearing the music and doing the motions with the big kids!

DAILY CHALLENGE™

During Sing & Play Roar, kids will have a chance to talk with their Cub Crew Leaders about how they completed the Daily Challenge. Look for ways preschoolers are living out the Bible Point each day during Serengeti Trek. Help them discover the joy of getting wild about God!

When the preschoolers are dismissed, tell the children to hold on to their lion tails with their Cub Crews and go to the Lion Cub Club room.

WILD WELCOME

(up to 10 minutes)

When the children arrive in your room, make sure each child is wearing his or her name badge. You can expect new children to visit Lion Cub Club each day, so have extra name badges on hand. Assign new children to Cub Crews that have fewer than five children in them. If most of your crews are full, check with the Serengeti Trek Director to see if he or she has recruited extra volunteers who might be available as Cub Crew Leaders.

SAY: It's so good to see all your smiling faces here at Lion Cub Club! Some of your crews may have new friends in them. Be sure to learn each person's name. Let's welcome each other while we sing!

Have the children sing the welcoming song "I'm So Glad" to the tune of "Ten Little Indians." Lead the children in greeting their friends and doing the motions.

I'm so glad my friends are here. *(Shake hands with a friend.)*

I'm so glad my friends are here. *(Shake hands with a friend.)*

I'm so glad my friends are here *(shake hands with a friend)*

At Ser-en-ge-ti Trek!

Roar!

I'm so glad my friends are here. *(Shake hands with a friend.)*

I'm so glad my friends are here. *(Shake hands with a friend.)*

I'm so glad my friends are here *(shake hands with a friend)*

At Ser-en-ge-ti Trek!

Roar!

Point to the Day 1 Bible Story poster, and **ASK:**

- **What do you remember about Gideon fighting the mean, mad Midianites?** (He used lights; he scared the bad guys; God helped him.)

SAY: Gideon knew God, and we can 📖 know God too. ("Wow!")

Point to the Day 2 Bible Story poster. **ASK:**

- **What do you remember about Daniel?** (He prayed; he was in a lions' den; he didn't get eaten by the lions.)

SAY: Daniel prayed three times each day. Daniel talked to God, and we can 📖 talk to God too. ("Wow!")

Point to the Day 3 Bible Story poster. **SAY:** Today's Bible story is about three friends who told a mean king about God. We'll see that you and I can 📖 tell about God ("Wow!") just as they did.

BIBLE STORY EXPEDITION

(up to 15 minutes)

Give each crew leader about ten blocks, four craft sticks, and a couple of sheets of red, orange, and yellow tissue paper. Open a Bible to Daniel 3:1-30, and show the passage to the children.

SAY: Our story comes from the Bible, God's special book, so we know it's true.

There once was a king with a silly, long name. His name was Nebuchadnezzar. I told you it was silly! Can you say that name with me?

Lead children in saying "Nebuchadnezzar." **Now let's say it three times fast.** Lead children in saying "Nebuchadnezzar" three times fast.

One day, Nebuchadnezzar woke up with the most ridiculous idea. He said, "I think I'll make a gold statue. I'll make it a god of gold! And I'll make it very, very tall. Everyone will have to look waaaaay up to see it."

HINTS FROM THE HERD

Kids really had trouble saying the names of today's Bible characters. We heard things like Shamrock, Merlock, and Bingo! (And that doesn't even count what we heard for Nebuchadnezzar!) Simplify things by calling them "the three friends" as much as possible. The names of these brave friends aren't nearly as important as what they did.

DAY 3

DAY 3

HINTS FROM THE HERD

This was a noisy and busy Bible story, but the preschoolers loved it! They were really engaged and interested, plus they enjoyed building, crumpling, and acting out the story. No fidgety kids here!

Direct each crew to use the blocks to build a statue near them. **Nebuchadnezzar wanted his people to look up and see a god of gold.** Point to the block statues. **Are these statues God? No! I don't think Nebuchadnezzar had such a good idea, do you? "And that's not all," thought Nebuchadnezzar. "When special music starts to play, all my people will kneel and worship this statue."** Have the children join you in singing, "la, la, la, la, la."

Would you want to bow to a statue? Shake your head. **I wouldn't. "Anyone who doesn't bow to my statue will get thrown into a fiery furnace," the king declared. That sounds really scary!**

Three friends who loved God lived in Nebuchadnezzar's land. Their names were Shadrach, Meshach, and Abednego. They worshipped the true God who made the heavens and earth and everything else. "This statue made of gold is no god," they said, "and we won't worship it." Lead children in pointing to the block statues and shaking their heads back and forth.

The three friends knew that they might get thrown into a hot, hot fire. But they were very brave. They said, "We'll only bow to the one true God." So when the music played, everyone bowed down to the statue...except the three friends. Tell children to turn their backs to the block statue and say, "No way!"

The king was so angry that he called the three friends to come talk to him. They told him about God. "Our God will save us," they said. "God will rescue us!" Well, that made the king *really* mad. He was so mad that he had the soldiers make the fire even hotter!

Let each crew tear down its statue and build a furnace (a large circle of blocks). Allow children to crumple red, orange, and yellow tissue paper and toss it into the middle of the block furnace.

SAY: When the fire was blazing hot, the soldiers tied up the three friends and threw them into the furnace. Let crews each place three craft sticks into the furnace. **Then a strange thing happened. King Nebuchadnezzar noticed something as he watched the fire. "Wait, didn't we put in *three* men? But now I see *four* men in the fire."** Direct crew leaders to add a fourth craft stick. **"And the fourth one looks like he's from heaven! None of them are even tied up—they're just walking around as if the fire doesn't even hurt!"**

So the king had his soldiers get the three friends out of the fire. Have children take the craft sticks from the furnace. **When Shadrach, Meshach, and Abednego stood before the king, not one hair on their heads was burned. They didn't even smell like smoke! Well, the king was so excited that he praised God! He even made a new law that said no one could say anything bad about God. Wow! He wanted everyone to tell about God.** ("Wow!")

Collect the blocks, and direct Cub Crews to sit in tight, knee-to-knee circles. Give each Cub Crew Leader a copy of the "Day 3: Talk About It" questions.

DAY 3: TALK ABOUT IT

- Why didn't Shadrach, Meshach, and Abednego worship the statue? (It wasn't God; they didn't love it; they knew it was wrong.)
- How do you think the three friends felt when King Nebuchadnezzar told them he was going to throw them in the furnace? (Afraid; sad; angry.)
- How did God help the three friends? (He made them not get burned up; God sent an angel.)

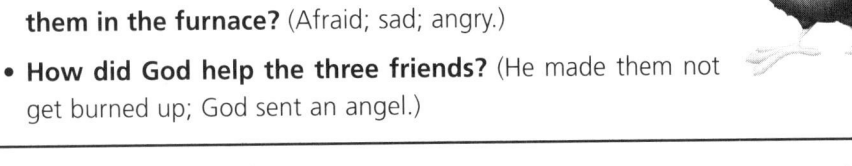

Permission to photocopy these questions from Group's Serengeti Trek: Lion Cub Club Preschool Director Manual granted for local church use. Copyright © Group Publishing, Inc., P.O. Box 481, Loveland, CO 80539. www.groupvbs.com

SAY: The three friends told the king about their mighty God. They said that God would save them. When God rescued Shadrach, Meshach, and Abednego, even the king wanted people to tell about God. Our Treasure Verse for today says, "I will tell of all the marvelous things you have done" (Psalm 9:1b). "Marvelous" is a big word for neat or great. So this means we'll talk about all the amazing, wonderful, cool things God does!

Let's stand up and sing a song with the words to our Treasure Verse. (Sing to the tune of "Did You Ever See a Lassie?")

I will tell of all the marvelous

Things God has done.

I will tell of all the marvelous

Things God has done!

Let children call out good things God has done, such as heal family members or create a wonderful world. Then sing the song again.

DAY 3

CUB CLUB CRAFT PLAY

(up to 30 minutes)

OPTION 1: WILDLIFE PHOTO FRAMES

1. With the children, look through a few books that have pictures of African animals. Talk about how God made all the beautiful animals. Explain that we can tell people how awesome God is to create animals like that.

2. Let children choose which photo frame they'd like to make—a zebra, a giraffe, or a cheetah. Distribute the frames, and write each child's name on the back of his or her frame.

3. Help children attach the spots or stripes to their frames. Talk about how beautiful the animals are and how "marvelous" they look. Use a Glue Dot to attach a magnet to the back of each photo frame. (The adhesive won't hold the magnet in place.)

4. As children work, **SAY:** **God is so amazing! Looking at these pretty patterns makes me want to tell about God.** ("Wow!") Encourage kids to put pictures of themselves in the frames since they are marvelous creations of God!

OPTION 2: APPEARING ANGEL

1. Give each child the Day 3 Bible Activity page from his or her Cub Club Bible Book, and write the child's name on his or her paper.

2. *Before children work on their Bible Activity pages,* turn them over and discuss the Daily Challenge with them. (The paint may be too wet to do this after children work on the paper.) Be sure each child chooses and circles the Challenge he or she will accomplish.

3. Tell children to each use a white crayon to draw an angel near the three friends in the furnace. Then direct children to create flames all around the furnace with watercolor paints. The angel will miraculously "appear"!

4. Remind children that God protected the three friends and even sent an angel to be with them in the furnace. Point out that when God does wonderful things for us, we can tell about God like Shadrach, Meshach, and Abednego.

HINTS FROM THE HERD

We had to help the three-year-olds press down a bit harder with the white crayons while they drew on the page. Encourage kids of all ages to press down so the white drawing will show up well against the "fiery flames."

Permission to photocopy these options from Group's Serengeti Trek: Lion Cub Club Preschool Director Manual granted for local church use. Copyright © Group Publishing, Inc., P.O. Box 481, Loveland, CO 80539. www.groupvbs.com

DAY 3

OPTION 3: TALK-A-PHONE

1. Cut a slit from the edge of each plate to the center.

2. Encourage children to decorate the back side of the plate with stickers and markers.

3. Roll the plate into a cone shape to look like a megaphone. Snip a hole at the end. Staple the ends securely.

4. Direct the children to talk through their talk-a-phones and say the Treasure Verse: "I will tell of all the marvelous things you have done" (Psalm 9:1b). Remind children that the three friends in today's Bible story told the king about God. We can 📖 tell about God too.

HINTS FROM THE HERD

We found that the cheapest white paper plates worked great since they rolled into the megaphone shape most easily.

OPTION 4: ON FIRE FOR GOD

1. Set out the blocks, tissue paper, and craft sticks used in Bible Story Expedition.

2. Let children use the items to build the statue then tear it down to make a furnace with the three friends (and an angel) inside.

3. Point out that the three friends told the king about God because they loved God so much. Encourage children to practice telling others about God.

Permission to photocopy these options from Group's Serengeti Trek: Lion Cub Club Preschool Director Manual granted for local church use. Copyright © Group Publishing, Inc., P.O. Box 481, Loveland, CO 80539. www.groupvbs.com

After about seventeen to twenty minutes, shake the tic tac drum, and announce that it's time for the children to finish their activities and clean up. When cleanup is complete, use your tic tac drum again, and wait for the children to gather in their Cub Crews.

SAY: It's time to watch our Chadder video to see what's happening with that crazy chipmunk.

ASK: • What do you remember about Chadder's adventure? (He's in Africa; there's a bad guy chasing him; he's supposed to deliver medicine.)

SAY: Chadder and Jabari are trying to get the medicine to Dr. Kim, but sneaky Dr. Gallstone wants the medicine too. Chadder was worried that lions would eat him while they camped in the Serengeti overnight. Let's see what happens to Chadder and Jabari.

DAY 3

CHADDER'S ADVENTURE THEATER

(up to 15 minutes)

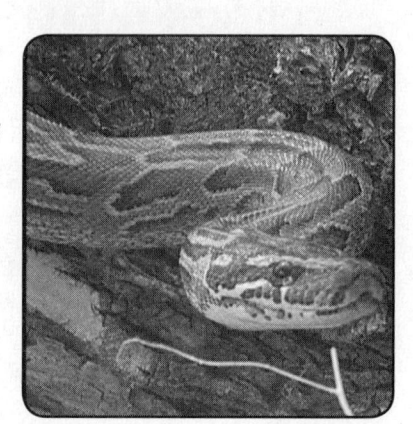

Lead the children to the place where you've set up a TV and a VCR or DVD player in your classroom, and let the children watch today's portion of *Chadder's Serengeti Trek Adventure*. When the video segment ends, turn off the VCR.

SAY: It looks like Chadder is in trouble, kind of like our friends Shadrach, Meshach, and Abednego.
ASK:

- **What should Chadder do?** (Run from the snake; get some help; pray.)

- **Do you think Chadder will get the medicine to Dr. Kim? Why or why not?** (No, Dr. Gallstone will get it; yes, God will help him.)

- **In this movie, who should Chadder tell about God?** (Dr. Gallstone; Dr. Kim; everyone.)

WATERING HOLE SNACKS

(up to 15 minutes)

Have the children sit at tables or in another eating area. Show children the snack, and point out that it looks like the three friends—and an angel—in the fiery furnace. Point out that they all look nice and cool in that furnace!

Lead the children in a simple prayer of thanksgiving. Then give each child a napkin or paper towel, a snack, and a cup half-filled with water. Keep handy a supply of wet wipes for kids to clean their hands and paper towels to wipe up any spills. When the children have finished their snacks, have them throw away their cups and other trash. Shake the tic tac drum and **SAY: It's time to learn about Operation Kid-to-Kid and then go to our Preschool Playtime stations.**

OPERATION KID-TO-KID™

(up to 5 minutes)

Have the Cub Crews gather near the Operation Kid-to-Kid poster. **SAY: Let's meet a new friend from Africa!** Point to the poster of Ajani, and read the information at the bottom. **Today we're learning to tell about God.** ("Wow!")
ASK:

- **What is something you could tell Ajani about God?** (That God loves him; that God is kind; that God is powerful.)

SAY: I love hearing you tell about God! ("Wow!") **You can help people know more about God through**

74 WWW.GROUPVBS.COM

what you *do,* too. **This week we're telling about God and sharing God's love through a special sharing project. All week long, we're collecting school supplies to send to children in Africa. Kids like Ajani will learn about God through the cool school supplies you bring in. Did anyone bring any school supplies today?**

Let children bring up any school supplies they've brought and place them in the boxes you've set out. Quickly count the number of items you've collected. **SAY: Wow! We have (number of items) school supplies collected! You are all super sharers! Sharing is a great way to tell about God.** ("Wow!")

PRESCHOOL PLAYTIME

(up to 15 minutes)

Take children outdoors, have them visit their favorite Cub Club Craft Play stations again, or let them engage in unstructured play. If you choose to go outdoors, intersperse some of the following activities with unstructured play.

DAY 3

OPTION 1: FOUR IN THE FIRE

Have children join hands and form a circle. Choose four children to stand in the middle of the circle "furnace." Give the rest of the kids red or orange crepe-paper streamers to wave. Lead kids in the following chant:

> Nebuchadnezzar threw in three.
> But I count four! How can that be?
> One, two, three, four!
> Come on out;
> Let's play some more.

Choose four other children to be inside the "fire," and repeat the game.

Talk about how God sent an angel to be with the three friends in the fire. Point out that God did an awesome thing by saving the three friends.

TREK TIPS

If preschoolers haven't made megaphones, simply roll construction paper into cones to create megaphones they can use.

OPTION 2: TALK-A-THON

Lead children in singing the Treasure Verse into the megaphones they made during Cub Club Craft Play. (Sing to the tune of "Did You Ever See a Lassie?")

I will tell of all the marvelous

Things God has done.

I will tell of all the marvelous

Things God has done!

At the end of each verse, remind children that we have learned to 🔖 tell about God. Encourage each crew member to tell about a great thing God has done for him or her.

Permission to photocopy these options from Group's Serengeti Trek: Lion Cub Club Preschool Director Manual granted for local church use. Copyright © Group Publishing, Inc., P.O. Box 481, Loveland, CO 80539. www.groupvbs.com

OPTION 3: PASS THE WORD

Form a line with at least five feet between each player. Have the crew leader start by whispering something about God to the first person in line. Crew leaders might say "I love God" or "God is cool." The child will then run to the next player and whisper the message into his or her ear. Kids will continue to pass the message until it reaches the last person, who will shout the message to the crew leader. Point out how much fun it is to tell about God.

HINTS FROM THE HERD

We first passed the Bible Point: "Tell about God." Then we tried a few other phrases about God. Kids were so tuned in to the Point that they always changed our message to "Tell about God." That's OK. We're glad they got the Point!

OPTION 4: FREE PLAY

If you're outdoors, let the children play with outdoor toys, such as balls, soap bubbles, or sidewalk chalk. Children would also enjoy playing on outdoor playground equipment if it's available. If you're indoors, let the children play with classroom toys, such as blocks, stuffed animals, or a water table. As the children play, look for opportunities to review today's Point and Bible story.

Permission to photocopy these options from Group's Serengeti Trek: Lion Cub Club Preschool Director Manual granted for local church use. Copyright © Group Publishing, Inc., P.O. Box 481, Loveland, CO 80539. www.groupvbs.com

After about fifteen minutes, shake your tic tac drum to let the children know it's time to finish their activities and clean up. When cleanup is complete, use your tic tac drum again. Have the children join their Cub Crews and gather in the Bible story area for Bible Memory Buddies.

DAY 3

BIBLE MEMORY BUDDIES

(up to 10 minutes)

Hold up an Elaine the Crane Bible Memory Buddy.

SAY: This is my friend Elaine the Crane. Cranes are tall birds that live in Africa. What sound do you think Elaine might make? Let children "perform" their suggestions. **Cranes talk and chatter a lot. Let's pretend we're cranes talking and chattering together.** Let crews "chatter" as if they're a flock of cranes. Shake your tic tac drum.

SAY: We can be chatterbox cranes too! We can 📖 tell about God—talking to our families, our friends, our neighbors…everyone! Crew leaders, when you hand out these cute cranes, remind your kids to 📖 tell about God!

Distribute Bible Memory Buddies to each crew leader, and direct them to hand one to each child, saying, "Now [child's name] can tell of all the marvelous things God has done!" Close by singing the Treasure Verse to the tune of "Did You Ever See a Lassie?"

I will tell of all the marvelous

Things God has done.

I will tell of all the marvelous

Things God has done!

Direct the Cub Crew Leaders to collect the children's crafts from Cub Club Craft Play to take to The Mane Event, shake the tic tac drum, and have the children assemble in their Cub Crews.

THE MANE EVENT

(up to 20 minutes)

Lead the children to The Mane Event. The Mane Event Leader will greet the children and show them where to sit. During The Mane Event, preschoolers will help create a fiery furnace and share things that make it hard—and easy—to tell about God.

When the Mane Event Leader dismisses everyone, have the preschoolers remain seated with their Cub Crew Leaders until parents or caregivers arrive to pick up their children. This is a good time for Cub Crew Leaders to collect the children's name badges and put them in the Crew Bags.

Remind the children to take today's Bible Activity page and other projects with them when they leave. Be sure to thank parents and caregivers for bringing their children to Serengeti Trek.

SAFARI SING-ALONG

Preschoolers love to sing, so here are a few songs you can intersperse with your activities. Sing these songs while kids are traveling, playing, waiting in line for the restroom, eating snacks, or when you just happen to have a few extra minutes.

These songs will remind kids to tell about God.

IN THE FIRE
(Sing to the tune of "Frère Jacques.")

In the fire,
In the fire,
Blazing hot!
Blazing hot!
Three friends didn't burn up.
Three friends didn't burn up.
They did not!
They did not!

I LIKE TO TELL
(Sing to the tune of "I've Got the Joy.")

I like to tell about
All my God has done,
My God has done,
My God has done!
I like to tell about
All my God has done.
My God is marvelous!

THREE GOOD FRIENDS
(Sing to the tune of "Three Blind Mice.")

Three good friends,
Three good friends,
They wouldn't bow.
They wouldn't bow.
Into the fire they had to go,
But God sent an angel to help, you know.
The king was amazed, and he let them go,
Those three good friends,
Three good friends.

Permission to photocopy this handout from Group's Serengeti Trek: Lion Cub Club Preschool Director Manual granted for local church use.
Copyright © Group Publishing, Inc., P.O. Box 481, Loveland, CO 80539. www.groupvbs.com

LION CUB CLUB
PRESCHOOL DIRECTOR MANUAL

DAY 4

BIBLE POINT:
Love God.

BIBLE STORY:
Jesus dies and rises again (John 19:1–20:18).

TREASURE VERSE:
"We love because God first loved us" (1 John 4:19).

If anyone had reason to love God wholeheartedly, it was Mary Magdalene. Luke 8:2 says that Jesus freed Mary from the bondage of *seven* demons. She went from living a life of despair to a life of hope and acceptance. Mary understood the power of God, and she also felt the compassion of Christ. She'd experienced Jesus' gentleness, forgiveness, and grace. So when Jesus died on the cross, it's likely that Mary felt her world crashing down around her. Her beloved Jesus was dead. Imagine her astonishment when, three days later in front of an empty tomb, Jesus appeared and lovingly spoke her name.

The word "love" is often overused by kids. "I love ice cream!" "I love playing soccer!" But God's love goes deeper than words can even describe. It's a relationship built from grace and compassion, mixed with forgiveness and devotion. And over all of that, God poured out the blood of his Son, Jesus. Today you have the opportunity to help kids catch a glimpse of that powerful love. Some children may already proclaim a love for God. Use the activities in your lesson to draw children into a deeper, more intimate relationship with God.

Because I love God, I will

- make choices that please God,
- make God a part of my everyday life,
- discover the power of worship, and
- find ways to share God's love with others.

LION CUB CLUB SCHEDULE

DAY 4

LOCATION	ACTIVITY	MINUTES	WHAT CHILDREN WILL DO	SUPPLIES
Sing & Play Roar	Sing & Play Roar	up to 25	Sing Serengeti Trek songs with the older children.	Name badges, lion tails
Lion Cub Club	Wild Welcome	up to 10	Greet their classmates, and sing a welcoming song.	Name badges, tic tac drum, Bible Story posters
Lion Cub Club	Bible Story Expedition	up to 15	Search for treasure, then discover clues to learn how Mary loved Jesus.	Bible, paper lunch sacks, plastic Easter eggs, chenille wires, paper, small stones, white fabric scraps, glitter, glue
Lion Cub Club	Cub Club Craft Play	up to 20	**Option 1: Wild Wobblers**—Make zany friends who are wild about God.	Wild Wobblers, round Chinet paper plates, markers
			Option 2: Heart-to-Heart—Put heart stickers on the activity page, and talk about the Daily Challenge.	Cub Club Bible Books, heart stickers, crayons
			Option 3: What Do I Love?—Make dough sculptures of things they love.	Modeling dough
			Option 4: Mystery Voice—Guess which child says, "I love God."	
Lion Cub Club	Chadder's Adventure Theater	up to 15	Discover how Chadder escapes a snake and loses the important medicine.	TV/VCR or TV/DVD player, *Chadder's Serengeti Trek Adventure* video
Watering Hole Snacks or Lion Cub Club	Watering Hole Snacks	up to 15	Eat Lovable Giraffes to remember how God reached out to us with love.	Snacks provided by the Watering Hole Snacks Leader, paper towels, cups of water, wet wipes
Lion Cub Club	Operation Kid-to-Kid	up to 5	Meet Muna, and count the number of school supply items they've collected.	Operation Kid-to-Kid poster
Lion Cub Club or outside	Preschool Playtime	up to 15	**Option 1: Blobs of Love**—Shout out their love for God, then tag friends.	
			Option 2: If You Love God—Sing a song and do silly motions to show the joy of loving God.	
			Option 3: Giraffe Laughs—Pretend to be giraffes.	Pool noodles
			Option 4: Free Play—Enjoy free play outdoors or in the classroom.	Playground equipment, various outdoor toys, classroom toys
Lion Cub Club	Bible Memory Buddies	up to 10	Reach high to receive treats, then receive a Bible Memory Buddy.	Candy or stickers, Gigi Bible Memory Buddies
The Mane Event	The Mane Event	up to 20	Sing songs, and receive stickers.	

LION CUB CLUB PREPARATIONS

DAY 4

Before the children arrive:

- For Bible Story Expedition, prepare a treasure bag for each Cub Crew and one bag for the Bible Story Expedition leader to use as an example. You'll need five plastic Easter eggs for each treasure bag. Place the following items in the eggs:

    Egg 1—a small paper heart

    Egg 2—a small paper circle with a grouchy face drawn on it

    Egg 3—a little cross made from two chenille wires

    Egg 4—a small rock (no smaller than a fifty-cent piece)

    Egg 5—a scrap of white fabric decorated with sequin dust or glitter

    Be sure to identify the eggs by number or color so crew leaders will be able to open them in the right order. Place five eggs in a paper lunch sack, and fold down the top. Hide the bags around the room.

- Choose the Cub Club Craft Play activities you'll use, photocopy the instructions, and collect and prepare the supplies. Set up each station as shown, and cover the supplies with a sheet.

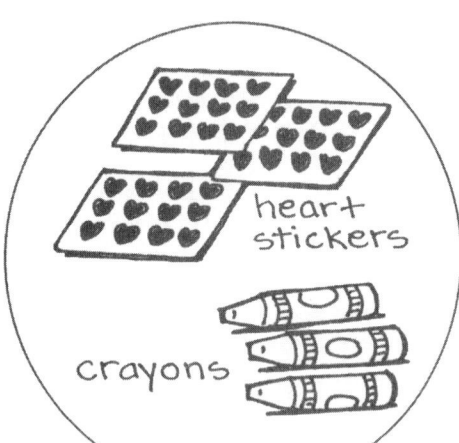

HINTS FROM THE HERD

We originally tried this with only three eggs, but the preschool director noted that each child really wanted to open an egg. So we've added two items for children to "find." We also used clear plastic eggs, which we had on hand, but we discovered that it was too distracting for kids to see the surprises waiting in the eggs. Using regular opaque Easter eggs works best. If you have trouble locating plastic Easter eggs in the summer, you can find them at www.groupoutlet.com.

Wild Wobblers — Chinet plates, Wild Wobblers markers

Heart-to-Heart — heart stickers, crayons

What Do I Love? — modeling dough

DAY 4

- Choose the Preschool Playtime activities you'll use, photocopy the instructions, collect the supplies you'll need, and set out the supplies next to the play areas.

- Hang up the Day 4 Bible Story poster with the previous days' posters on a wall near your Bible Story Expedition area.

- Check with the Watering Hole Snacks Leader to find out what time the Service Crew will deliver your snacks or if you will go to Watering Hole Snacks.

- Hang up today's Operation Kid-to-Kid poster in your Bible Story Expedition area. Today children will meet Muna.

- Post a sign on your door letting parents know that children will meet their Cub Crew Leaders at Sing & Play Roar.

SING & PLAY ROAR

(up to 25 minutes)

Before the children arrive, arrange with the Sing & Play Roar Leader to reserve seats up front for your preschoolers. Plan to have a specific area for each Cub Crew. That way, if some kids arrive late, they'll know where to look for their crews.

Greet the children as they arrive, and have Cub Crew Leaders give the children their name badges. Have Cub Crew Leaders collect any school supplies children have brought and place them in Crew Bags. (They can drop off the supplies in your designated Operation Kid-to-Kid area when they return to Lion Cub Club.) The crew leaders can sit with children and involve them in this worship time. Preschoolers will enjoy hearing the music and doing the motions with the big kids!

DAILY CHALLENGE™

During Sing & Play Roar, kids will have a chance to talk with their crew leaders about how they completed the Daily Challenge. Look for ways preschoolers are living out the Bible Point each day during Serengeti Trek. Help them discover the joy of getting wild about God!

After the kids have been dismissed, tell the children to hold on to the lion tails with their Cub Crews and go to the Lion Cub Club room.

WILD WELCOME

(up to 10 minutes)

When the children arrive in your room, make sure each child is wearing his or her name badge. You can expect new children to visit Lion Cub Club each day, so have extra name badges on hand. Assign new children to Cub Crews that have fewer than five children in them. If most of your crews are full, check with the Serengeti Trek Director to see if he or she has recruited extra volunteers who might be available as Cub Crew Leaders.

SAY: It's so good to see all your smiling faces here at Lion Cub Club! Let's welcome each other while we sing!

DAY 4

Have the children sing the welcoming song "I'm So Glad" to the tune of "Ten Little Indians." Lead the children in greeting their friends and doing the motions.

I'm so glad my friends are here. *(Shake hands with a friend.)*

I'm so glad my friends are here. *(Shake hands with a friend.)*

I'm so glad my friends are here *(shake hands with a friend)*

At Ser-en-ge-ti Trek!

Roar!

I'm so glad my friends are here. *(Shake hands with a friend.)*

I'm so glad my friends are here. *(Shake hands with a friend.)*

I'm so glad my friends are here *(shake hands with a friend)*

At Ser-en-ge-ti Trek!

Roar!

SAY: **Let's see if you can say our Bible Points with me. Your crew leaders will shout "Wow!"**

Point to the Day 1 Bible Story poster, and lead children in saying, "Know God!" Pause while crew leaders say "Wow!" **We learned how Gideon knew and trusted God to help him fight a big army.**

Point to the Day 2 Bible Story poster, and lead children in saying, "Talk to God!" Pause while crew leaders say "Wow!" **This picture reminds us of how Daniel prayed and talked to God.**

Point to the Day 3 Bible Story poster, and lead children in saying, "Tell about God!" Pause while crew leaders say "Wow!" **These three friends talked about God, even when they were thrown into a hot fire.**

Point to the Day 4 Bible Story poster. **SAY: Let's get ready to hear how much God loves us and how we can love God.** ("Wow!")

BIBLE STORY EXPEDITION

(up to 15 minutes)

Open your Bible to John 19, and show it to the children. **SAY: Our Bible story comes from the book of John in the Bible. The story is about God's special son, Jesus. God sent Jesus to live on the Earth to tell people about God and to show them how much God loves us. Jesus was a special treasure sent to us from God. We'll start today by having a treasure hunt!**

Direct Cub Crews to stay together as they each search for a treasure bag. When a Cub Crew finds a bag, have the Cub Crew Leader keep the bag shut and gather crew members together. When every crew has a bag and is seated, continue. **ASK:**

- **What was it like to search for your treasure bag?** (Fun; exciting; hard.)

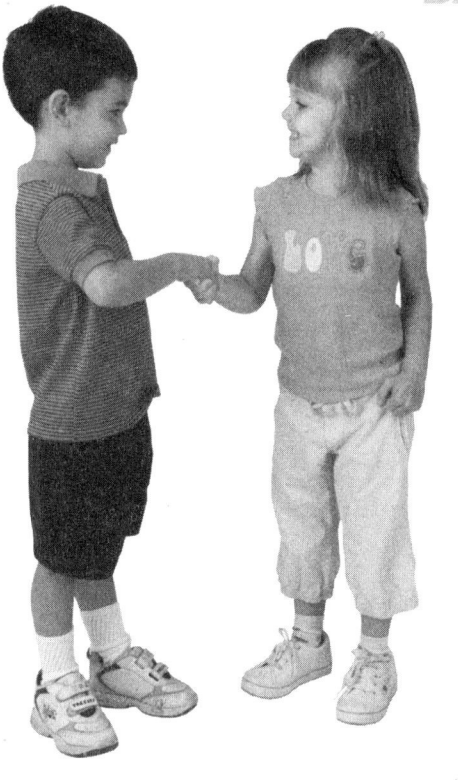

TREK TIPS

Be sure to have crew leaders hold each item (and the eggs) as children open the eggs. Keep distractions out of the children's hands so they can focus on the Bible story and discussion.

DAY 4

- **How did you feel when you found your crew's treasure bag?** (Glad; happy; excited.)

SAY: Today we'll hear about someone who was looking for a treasure. Her name was Mary. Let's see if we can learn more about Mary and her treasure—Jesus!

Let's open these treasures one at a time to see what they tell us about Jesus. Direct crew leaders to each take out the first egg and allow a child to open it. Ask children to tell you what's inside the egg. **This heart reminds us that Mary loved Jesus. Jesus was a good friend to Mary—he helped her when others were unkind to her. Jesus showed Mary how much God loved her too.**

To remember that Jesus and Mary were friends, hug a friend in your crew. Pause while crew members give hugs.

I wonder what else is in the bag. Direct crew leaders to each take out the second egg and let a child open it. Ask children to tell you what's inside. Hold up the grouchy face. **Jesus taught people about God. He showed God's power by healing people or even feeding them. Lots of people liked what Jesus said, but other people didn't. Some people were angry with Jesus. They thought he was lying when he said he was God's special Son. ASK:**

- **What does your face look like when *you're* angry?** Let children show you their mad faces. **SAY:** Oh my! You look just like the angry crowd that Jesus faced long ago.

Let's see what our next treasure tells us about Jesus. Direct crew leaders to each take out the third egg and allow a child to open it. Ask children to tell you what's inside the egg. **One day, some men took Jesus away. They didn't like the things Jesus said. They were so angry that they hurt Jesus and put him on a cross like this.** Hold up your little cross. **Jesus died to take away all the bad things we do. This cross reminds us that Jesus loved you so much that he died so you could live forever with God. ASK:**

- **How do you think Mary felt when Jesus died on the cross?** (Sad; mad.)

SAY: Maybe our next treasure will tell us what happened next. Direct crew leaders to each find the fourth egg and let a child open it. Ask children what they found inside. Hold up your rock. **After Jesus died, they wrapped up his body in soft cloths and put it in a cave called a tomb. They rolled a big, huge, gigantic stone over the opening of the cave. That way, no one could take Jesus' body away.**

A few days later, Mary went to the tomb. Our next treasure might help us know what happened there.

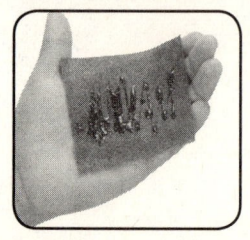

Direct crew leaders to each take out the last egg and allow a child to open it. Ask children to tell you what's inside the egg. **SAY:** When Mary went to the tomb, she got a big surprise. Instead of a cave with a huge rock in front of it, Mary saw a big cave...with a big rock lying on its side. The tomb was open! But Jesus' body wasn't there. Only a piece of cloth was inside the tomb. It was the cloth they'd wrapped Jesus' body in. **ASK:**

- How do you think Mary felt when she saw that Jesus wasn't in the tomb? (Weird; glad; sad.)

SAY: Mary was sad and scared when she discovered that Jesus' body was missing from the tomb. She didn't know that Jesus was alive again. Jesus was her friend—a treasure to her. She was afraid someone had taken him away. Just as you searched for your treasure bags, she was searching for her treasure—Jesus. Then Mary got an even bigger surprise. A man appeared and said her name. **Let's all call Mary together.** Lead children in calling "Mary!"

When Mary heard the voice, she realized it was Jesus! Jesus was alive! Mary was so happy and excited. I'm excited that Jesus is alive too. That's because I 📖 love God. ("Wow!") Even though it's sad that Jesus had to die on a cross, I'm glad he took away all the wrong things I do. I 📖 love God! ("Wow!") **Let's pray and tell God how much we love him.**

PRAY: Dear God, thank you for sending Jesus to show your love. Thank you for allowing Jesus to die and take away our sins. Thank you for your promise to take everyone who believes in you to heaven someday. We love you so much. In Jesus' name, amen.

DAY 4

CUB CLUB CRAFT PLAY

(up to 20 minutes)

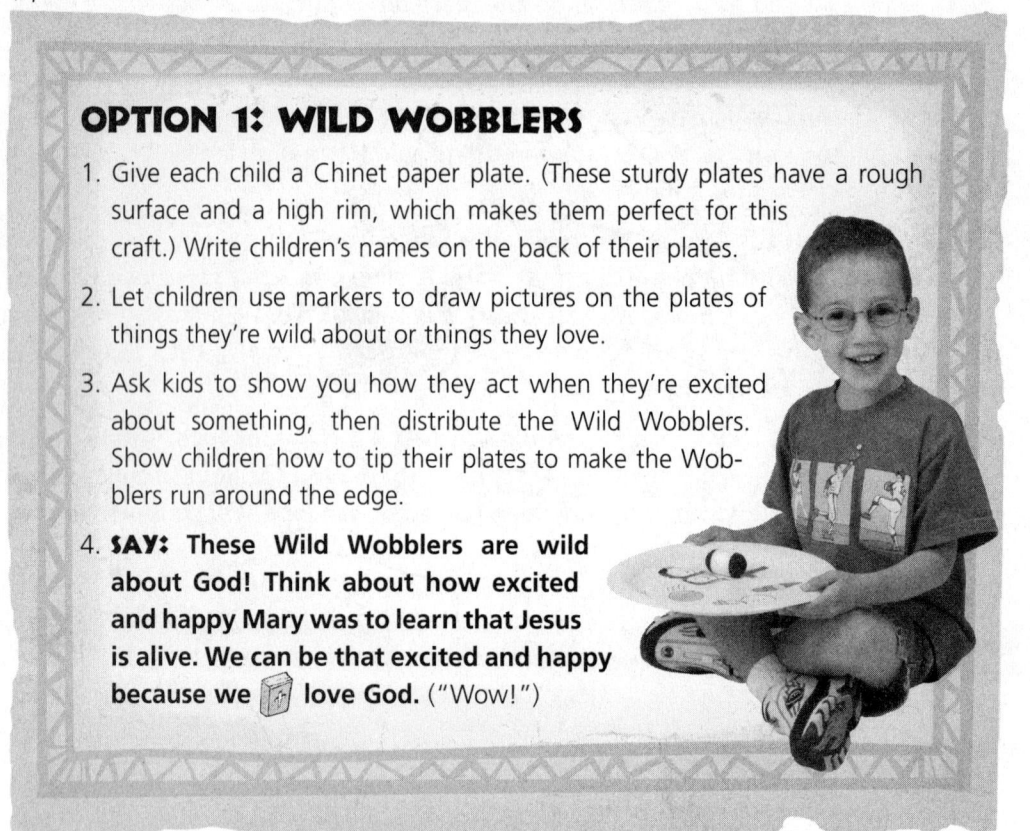

OPTION 1: WILD WOBBLERS

1. Give each child a Chinet paper plate. (These sturdy plates have a rough surface and a high rim, which makes them perfect for this craft.) Write children's names on the back of their plates.

2. Let children use markers to draw pictures on the plates of things they're wild about or things they love.

3. Ask kids to show you how they act when they're excited about something, then distribute the Wild Wobblers. Show children how to tip their plates to make the Wobblers run around the edge.

4. **SAY:** These Wild Wobblers are wild about God! Think about how excited and happy Mary was to learn that Jesus is alive. We can be that excited and happy because we 📖 love God. ("Wow!")

OPTION 2: HEART-TO-HEART

1. Tear out each child's Day 4 Bible Activity page from his or her Cub Club Bible Book. Write each child's name on his or her paper.

2. Direct children to place heart stickers between Mary and Jesus. Children can use crayons to color the picture of Mary and Jesus.

3. Remind children that Mary loved God and they can 📖 love God too.

4. Direct children to turn their pages over, and discuss the Daily Challenge opportunities with them. Help each child choose and circle the Challenge he or she will accomplish at home.

Permission to photocopy these options from Group's Serengeti Trek: Lion Cub Club Preschool Director Manual granted for local church use. Copyright © Group Publishing, Inc., P.O. Box 481, Loveland, CO 80539. www.groupvbs.com

DAY 4

OPTION 3: WHAT DO I LOVE?

1. Give each child a handful of modeling dough. Encourage children to each make a sculpture of something they love. Children might sculpt family members, pets, or hobbies they enjoy.

2. Talk about the things the kids love and how much God loves each of them.

3. **SAY:** I 📖 love God more than anything! ("Wow!") I'm glad God sent Jesus to take away my sins.

OPTION 4: MYSTERY VOICE

1. Form a circle, and remind children of how Mary recognized Jesus when he spoke to her.

2. Have children close their eyes. Tap one child on the head, and have that child open his or her eyes and move to the middle of the circle. The child should say, "I love God." Then have the child sit back down in the circle.

3. Children may open their eyes and guess who spoke. After three guesses, have the speaker say, "I love God!"

4. Repeat the game until everyone has had a chance to speak. You might make it tricky by telling the speaker to use a different voice when he or she talks.

5. Remind children that Mary loved God and we can 📖 love God too!

Permission to photocopy these options from Group's Serengeti Trek: Lion Cub Club Preschool Director Manual granted for local church use. Copyright © Group Publishing, Inc., P.O. Box 481, Loveland, CO 80539. www.groupvbs.com

After about seventeen to twenty minutes, shake the tic tac drum, and announce that it's time for the children to clean up Cub Club Craft Play and get ready to do some other fun activities. When cleanup is complete, use your tic tac drum again, and wait for the children to gather in their Cub Crews.

DAY 4

SAY: Now it's time to see what Chadder Chipmunk is up to. If I remember the story, Chadder was facing a giant snake who wanted to make him a snack! **ASK:**

- What do you think will happen to Chadder today? (He'll get the medicine to the kids; he'll meet another lion.)

SAY: I can't wait to see what Chadder discovers on the Serengeti today! I hope he gets the medicine to Dr. Kim, and I hope that Dr. Gallstone leaves him alone.

CHADDER'S ADVENTURE THEATER

(up to 15 minutes)

Lead the children to the place where you've set up a TV and a VCR or DVD player in your classroom, and let the children watch today's portion of *Chadder's Serengeti Trek Adventure*. When the segment ends, turn off the video. **ASK:**

- What has Chadder done to show that he loves God? (Talked about God with Jabari; prayed; is taking medicine to sick kids.)

SAY: Chadder is on a mission because he [] loves God. ("Wow!") I'll give you one minute to huddle with your crew and think of all the ways you might show others that *you* [] love God. ("Wow!") Ready? Go! Time crews for one minute.

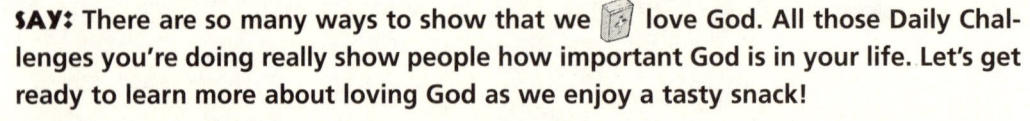

SAY: There are so many ways to show that we [] love God. All those Daily Challenges you're doing really show people how important God is in your life. Let's get ready to learn more about loving God as we enjoy a tasty snack!

WATERING HOLE SNACKS

(up to 15 minutes)

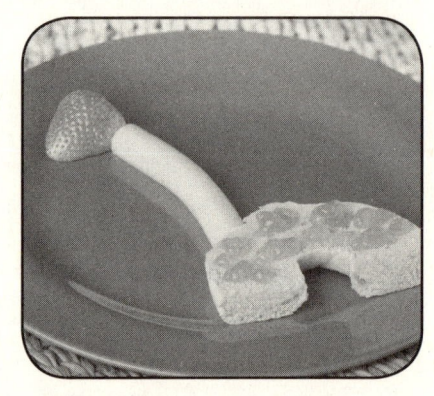

Have the children sit at tables or in another eating area. Hold up a snack, and point out that it looks like a giraffe. Tell children that giraffes have long necks that reach way up to the tops of trees. Point out that God loved us so much that he reached out to us by sending his Son, Jesus, to take away our sins.

Lead the children in a simple prayer of thanksgiving. Then give each child a napkin or paper towel, a snack, and a cup half-filled with water. Keep handy a supply of wet wipes for kids to clean their hands and paper towels to wipe up any spills. When the children have finished their snacks, have them throw away their cups and other trash. Shake your tic tac drum, and **SAY:** It's time to learn about Operation Kid-to-Kid and then go to Preschool Playtime.

OPERATION KID-TO-KID™

DAY 4

(up to 5 minutes)

Have the Cub Crews gather near the Operation Kid-to-Kid poster. **SAY:** I 📖 **love God, and I want to help others know and love God too.** ("Wow!") **Let's meet a new friend who we can share God's love with.** Point to the poster of Muna, and read the information at the bottom.

SAY: This week we're telling about God and sharing God's love all over the world through a special sharing project! All week long, we're collecting school supplies to send to children in Africa. Kids like Muna will learn about God through the cool school supplies you bring in. Did anyone bring any school supplies today?

Let children bring up any supplies they've brought and place them in the boxes in your room. Cheer for the kids who are coming forward, then quickly count the number of items you've collected. **SAY: Wow! We have** [number of items] **school supplies collected! God is so pleased by your sharing. Remember to bring your items tomorrow so we can make the school kits. They're an easy way to show that we** 📖 **love God.**

PRESCHOOL PLAYTIME

(up to 15 minutes)

Take children outdoors, have them visit their favorite Cub Club Craft Play stations again, or let them engage in unstructured play. If you choose to go outdoors, intersperse some of the following activities with unstructured play.

DAY 4

HINTS FROM THE HERD

Our leaders discovered that kids loved this game, although it really got them wound up. Follow this game with a lower-energy game like "Giraffe Laughs" to help kids wind down.

OPTION 1: BLOBS OF LOVE

Choose a crew leader and a child to stand in the middle of the playing area holding hands. Direct the rest of the children to line up on one side of the playing area. Have the people in the middle call, "We love God. Yes, we do! We love God. How 'bout you?" When the "callers" finish the chant, the rest of the children should race to the opposite side of the playing area. If the callers tag any children, those children should join them in the middle.

Continue the game until only one child is untagged. This child may choose a friend to join him or her in the middle for the next round.

OPTION 2: IF YOU LOVE GOD

Teach children the following song to the tune of "If You're Happy and You Know It."

If you love God and you know it, hug a friend. *(Hug a friend.)*

If you love God and you know it, hug a friend. *(Hug a different friend.)*

If you love God and you know it *(join hands and walk in a circle),*

Then your life will surely show it.

If you love God and you know it, hug a friend. *(Hug a different friend.)*

Sing the song again, filling in the following phrases for "hug a friend": jump for joy, dance around, shake a hand, shout "Hurray!"

Permission to photocopy these options from Group's Serengeti Trek: Lion Cub Club Preschool Director Manual granted for local church use. Copyright © Group Publishing, Inc., P.O. Box 481, Loveland, CO 80539. www.groupvbs.com

OPTION 3: GIRAFFE LAUGHS

Give each child a pool noodle, and have preschoolers hold the noodles over their heads as they pretend to be giraffes. Challenge children to see if their giraffes can "kiss" other giraffes by touching the ends of their pool noodles together.

Talk about how giraffes reach way up into the trees to find food. Point out that God reached out to us by sending his Son, Jesus, to take away our sins.

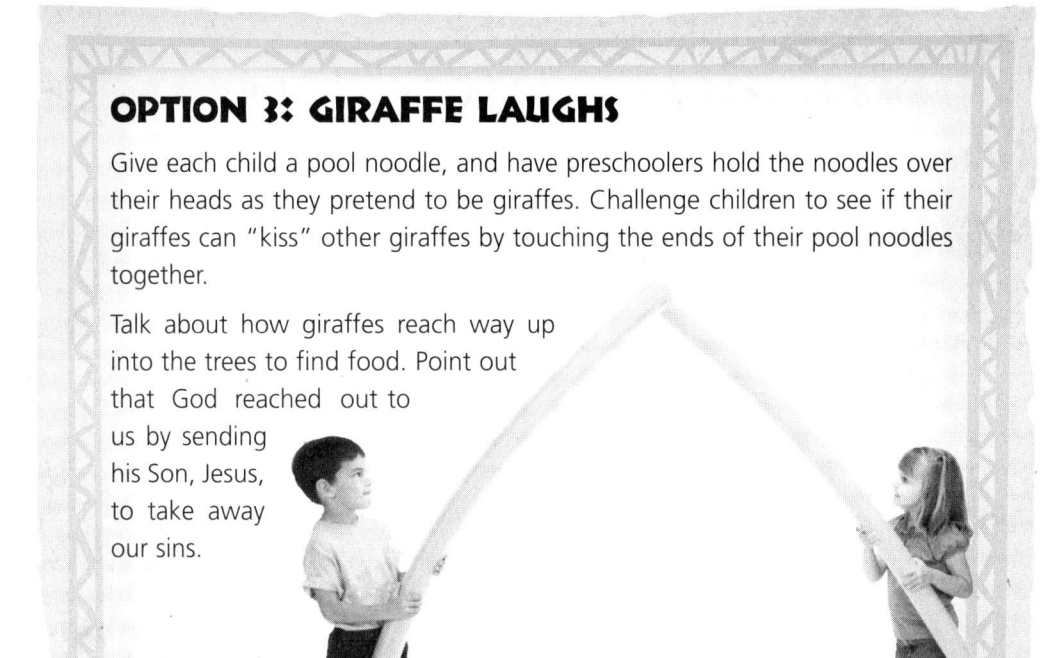

OPTION 4: FREE PLAY

If you're outdoors, let the children play with outdoor toys, such as balls, soap bubbles, or sidewalk chalk. Children would also enjoy playing on outdoor playground equipment if it's available. If you're indoors, let the children play with classroom toys, such as blocks, stuffed animals, or a water table. As the children play, look for opportunities to review today's Point and Bible story.

Permission to photocopy these options from Group's Serengeti Trek: Lion Cub Club Preschool Director Manual granted for local church use. Copyright © Group Publishing, Inc., P.O. Box 481, Loveland, CO 80539. www.groupvbs.com

After about fifteen minutes, shake the tic tac drum, and announce that it's time for the children to clean up Preschool Playtime and get ready to do some other fun activities. When cleanup is complete, use your tic tac drum again, and wait for the children to gather in their Cub Crews.

DAY 4

BIBLE MEMORY BUDDIES

(up to 10 minutes)

Give each crew leader a handful of candy or stickers, and direct crew leaders to hold the treats overhead. Ask children to try to get the treats by jumping or reaching as high as they can. **ASK:**

- **Why can't you get the treats?** (They're too high; I can't reach them.)
- **What would help you get the treats?** (If my crew leader gave me one; if I had a chair to stand on.)

Have crew leaders distribute the treats, then direct children to sit down while they enjoy them.

SAY: Just as you couldn't reach the treats, God knew that people could never reach heaven on their own. In order to be in heaven, we have to be perfect! We couldn't lie...not even once! We couldn't disobey our parents...ever! Those wrong things would keep us from living with God. So God reached out and gave us his precious Son, Jesus.

Our Treasure Verse today says, "We love because God first loved us" (1 John 4:19). Let's have fun singing about God's love.

Lead children in singing this song to the tune of "London Bridge." As children sing, have each Cub Crew do "London Bridge" motions.

We love since God first loved us,

First loved us,

First loved us.

We love since God first loved us. *(Lower arms to catch a child.)*

[Name of child], **love God!**

The child who is caught will respond with "Wow!"

Play a few times, catching as many children as you can. Then have crews gather again. Hold up a Gigi Bible Memory Buddy. **SAY: This is Gigi the Giraffe. Giraffes have these awesome long necks that remind me of the way God reached out to us. Giraffes are loving, gentle animals—that reminds me of God too. As your Cub Crew Leader gives you a Bible Memory Buddy, he or she will remind you of how much God loves you.**

Distribute Bible Memory Buddies, and have crew leaders hand one to each child while saying, "[Child's name], God loves you." Direct children to put the buddies in their Crew Bags. Have Cub Crew Leaders collect the children's crafts so they can distribute them to crew members before they are picked up by their parents. Have the children assemble in their Cub Crews and travel on their lion tails to The Mane Event.

THE MANE EVENT

DAY 4

(up to 20 minutes)

Lead the children to The Mane Event. The Mane Event Leader will greet the children and show them where to sit. In today's Mane Event, children will each receive a sticker and then have the opportunity to give the sticker to Jesus as a way to give their love to God.

When the Mane Event Leader dismisses everyone, have the preschoolers remain seated with their Cub Crew Leaders until parents or caregivers arrive to pick up their children. This is a good time for Cub Crew Leaders to collect the children's name badges and put the badges in the Crew Bags.

Remind the children to take today's Bible Activity page and other projects with them when they leave. Be sure to thank parents and caregivers for bringing their children to Serengeti Trek.

SAFARI SING-ALONG

Preschoolers love to sing, so here are a few songs you can intersperse with your activities. Sing these songs while kids are traveling, playing, waiting in line for the restroom, eating snacks, or when you just happen to have a few extra minutes.

These songs will remind kids to 📖 love God.

JESUS IS ALIVE
(Sing to the tune of "Jesus Loves Me.")

Jesus is alive today.

Jesus rose on the third day.

Jesus lives in heaven above.

I'll remember his great love.

Yes, I love Jesus.

Yes, I love Jesus.

Yes, I love Jesus.

I'll remember his great love.

I love Jesus. Does he know?

Have I ever told him so?

I will tell him every day,

In my work and in my play.

Yes, I love Jesus.

Yes, I love Jesus.

Yes, I love Jesus.

I'll tell him every day.

I LOVE GOD
(Sing to the tune of "Bingo.")

I love God, and God loves me.

We're forever friends!

I love God, and God loves me.

We're forever friends!

He sent his Son,

Who died for me.

I'll love him for eternity!

I love God, and God loves me.

We're forever friends!

WE LOVE GOD
(Sing to the tune of "Ten Little Indians.")

Which of my friends loves the Lord?

Which of my friends loves the Lord?

Which of my friends loves the Lord?

Let me call your name!

[Child's name], [Child's name] **loves the Lord!**

[Child's name], [Child's name] **loves the Lord!**

[Child's name], [Child's name] **loves the Lord!**

[Child's name], **he/she loves God!**

LION CUB CLUB
PRESCHOOL DIRECTOR MANUAL

DAY 5

BIBLE POINT:
Work for God.

BIBLE STORY:
Paul and Silas worship God in prison (Acts 16:16-40).

TREASURE VERSE:
Work hard and cheerfully as though for the Lord (adapted from Colossians 3:23).

Paul and Silas were not easily discouraged. Imagine being heckled day in and day out by a girl with a persistent evil spirit. Imagine the sense of injustice you'd feel if you were publicly blamed and humiliated for freeing her. Imagine being mobbed by an angry crowd, falsely accused, publicly stripped, severely beaten, and thrown into prison. It's easy to skim over the drastic circumstances of this story simply because we're so familiar with them. What would cause Paul and Silas to think of praising God when their bodies throbbed with pain and every sense was assaulted by their foul surroundings? Simply because they served God. And every action and word was a testimony and an offering to their heavenly Father.

While the kids who attend your VBS probably don't face the intense persecution that Paul and Silas experienced, kids *do* understand what it means to face challenges. It can be hard to get along with siblings every day. It's no fun to congratulate the winners when you're on the losing team. And it's certainly a challenge to give a friend a bigger piece of pizza—or even worse, the very last slice! But each of these difficulties can be put into perspective when we see it as a service to God. Today's activities will help you guide kids to discover the joy that comes when we give God our very best.

Because I work for God, I will

- do my best in service to God,
- look for opportunities to work for God every day,
- have the courage to do hard things, and
- talk and act like someone who serves God.

LION CUB CLUB SCHEDULE

DAY 5

LOCATION	ACTIVITY	MINUTES	WHAT CHILDREN WILL DO	SUPPLIES
Sing & Play Roar	Sing & Play Roar	up to 25	Sing Serengeti Trek songs with the older children.	name badges, lion tails
Lion Cub Club	Wild Welcome	up to 10	Greet their classmates, and sing a welcoming song.	name badges, tic tac drum, Bible Story posters
Lion Cub Club	Bible Story Expedition	up to 15	Make a rumbly earthquake, and explore the story of Paul and Silas in jail.	Bible, "Day 5: Talk About It" questions
Lion Cub Club	Cub Club Craft Play	up to 30	**Option 1: Lug's Water Blasters**—Make squirting toys to remember how elephants work hard.	Lug's Water Blaster Kits, scissors, markers, cups of water
			Option 2: Praise in Prison—Place bars on the jail, and talk about the Daily Challenge.	Cub Club Bible Books, glue, paper dessert plates, black chenille wires
			Option 3: Worship and Work—Make musical instruments for praising God.	Paper plates, markers, stickers, crepe-paper streamers, beans, stapler
			Option 4: Jailed for God—Go to "jail" and sing worship songs, then experience a noisy "earthquake."	Card table, black crepe paper, tape
Lion Cub Club	Chadder's Adventure Theater	up to 15	See how Chadder and Jabari get the medicine to the children.	TV/VCR or TV/DVD player, *Chadder's Serengeti Trek Adventure* video
Watering Hole Snacks or Lion Cub Club	Watering Hole Snacks	up to 15	Enjoy a snack that looks like Paul and Silas in prison.	Snacks provided by the Watering Hole Snacks Leader, paper towels, cups of water, wet wipes
Lion Cub Club	Operation Kid-to-Kid	up to 5	Count all the items they've collected for Operation Kid-to-Kid.	
Lion Cub Club or outside	Preschool Playtime	up to 20	**Option 1: Operation Kid-to-Kid Assembly**—Work together to create their Operation Kid-to-Kid school supply kits.	School supplies (from children), 1-gallon resealable plastic bags, *A Time for Everything* books (from Cub Club Bible Books)
			Option 2: Work Like an Elephant—Play a game with elephant trunks, and remember to work together as Paul and Silas did.	Pool noodles, lion tails, playground balls
			Option 3: Shake, Shake, Shake the Jailhouse—Play a game to depict the earthquake in the jailhouse.	
			Option 4: Free Play—Enjoy free play outdoors or in the classroom.	Playground equipment, various outdoor toys, classroom toys
Lion Cub Club	Bible Memory Buddies	up to 10	Use their "elephant trunks" to serve each other, and receive a Lug Bible Memory Buddy.	Lug Bible Memory Buddies
The Mane Event	The Mane Event	up to 20	Sing songs, and present their Operation Kid-to-Kid school supply kits.	

LION CUB CLUB PREPARATIONS

DAY 5

Before the children arrive:

- Photocopy the "Day 5: Talk About It" questions on page 105. You'll need one for each crew.

- Choose the Cub Club Craft Play activities you'll use, photocopy the instructions, and collect and prepare the supplies. Set up each station as shown, and cover the supplies with a sheet.

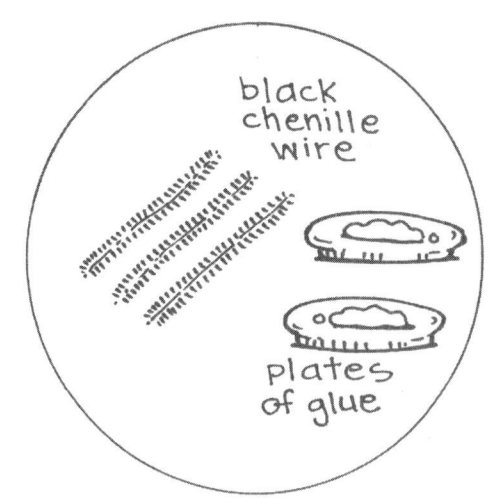

Lug's Water Blasters — markers, craft foam and stencil, scissors, cups of water

Praise in Prison — black chenille wire, plates of glue

Worship & Work — paper plates, crepe-paper streamers, uncooked beans, stapler

Jailed for God — Black crepe-paper streamers (all around table)

- Choose the Preschool Playtime activities you'll use, photocopy the instructions, collect the supplies you'll need, and set out the supplies next to the play areas.

- Hang up the Day 5 Bible Story poster with the previous days' posters on a wall near your Bible Story Expedition area.

- Check with the Watering Hole Snacks Leader to find out what time the Watering Hole Snacks Service Crew will deliver your snacks.

- Post a sign on your door letting parents know that the children are to meet their crews at Sing & Play Roar.

WWW.GROUPVBS.COM 99

DAY 5

SING & PLAY ROAR

(up to 25 minutes)

Before the children arrive, arrange with the Sing & Play Roar Leader to reserve seats up front for your preschoolers. Plan to have a specific area for each Cub Crew. That way, if some kids arrive late, they'll know where to look for their crews.

Greet the children as they arrive, and have the Cub Crew Leaders give the children their name badges. Have Cub Crew Leaders collect any school supplies children have brought and place them in their Crew Bags. (They can drop off the supplies in your designated Operation Kid-to-Kid area when they return to the Lion Cub Club classroom.) The crew leaders can sit with children and involve them in this worship time. Preschoolers will enjoy hearing the music and doing the motions with the big kids!

DAILY CHALLENGE™

During Sing & Play Roar, kids will have a chance to talk with their Cub Crew Leaders about how they completed the Daily Challenge. Look for ways preschoolers are living out the Bible Point each day during Serengeti Trek. Help them discover new ways to be wild about God!

After the kids have been dismissed, tell the children to hold on to the lion tails with their Cub Crews and go to the Lion Cub Club room.

WILD WELCOME

(up to 10 minutes)

When the children arrive in your room, make sure each child is wearing his or her name badge.

SAY: It's so good to see all your smiling faces here at Lion Cub Club! Let's welcome each other while we sing!

Have the children sing the welcoming song "I'm So Glad" to the tune of "Ten Little Indians." Lead the children in greeting their friends and doing the motions.

I'm so glad my friends are here. *(Shake hands with a friend.)*

I'm so glad my friends are here. *(Shake hands with a friend.)*

I'm so glad my friends are here *(shake hands with a friend)*

At Ser-en-ge-ti Trek!

Roar!

I'm so glad my friends are here. *(Shake hands with a friend.)*

I'm so glad my friends are here. *(Shake hands with a friend.)*

I'm so glad my friends are here *(shake hands with a friend)*

At Ser-en-ge-ti Trek!

Roar!

SAY: We've had a fun, busy week at Serengeti Trek. Let's see if you can remember all the things we've learned. Point to the Bible Story posters, and let children take turns coming up to the posters and telling about the Bible stories and Bible Points they've learned at Serengeti Trek.

Point to the Day 5 Bible Story poster. **SAY:** Today our Bible story is about two men named Paul and Silas. Paul and Silas loved Jesus and worked to tell everyone about God's love. Even though it was hard, they 📖 worked for God! ("Wow!") Let's find out what happened to Paul and Silas.

BIBLE STORY EXPEDITION

(up to 15 minutes)

Open a Bible to Acts 16:16-40, and show the passage to the children. **SAY:** Our story comes from the Bible, God's special book. Listen while I tell you about how Paul and Silas 📖 worked for God. ("Wow!")

Paul and Silas were two men who loved God very much. They walked to many places, telling people about Jesus. Let's be like Paul and Silas. Direct children to walk around the room and find three friends in different crews. Children should shake each other's hands and say, "God loves you!" After thirty seconds, shake your tic tac drum, and have children sit with their crews.

Many people who heard Paul and Silas believed in Jesus. One day, Paul and Silas helped a slave girl. Her masters got really angry, grabbed Paul and Silas, and dragged them away. The people began to hit Paul and Silas with sticks and tear their clothes. They had Paul and Silas arrested and thrown into jail. The jail guard pinned their feet down with large blocks of wood.

Let's grab each other's ankles and pin them down to see what it felt like for Paul and Silas. Demonstrate how you want children to sit. Have crew members form pairs and sit side by side, facing each other with their legs outstretched. Direct children to reach over and hold their friends' ankles.

Then the jail guard chained Paul and Silas with heavy chains. **ASK:**

- If you did something nice, then got beaten, yelled at, and thrown into jail, how would you feel and what would you do? Talk about that with your partner.

Allow children to share with their friends, then shake your tic tac drum, and ask a few children to share their answers.

SAY: Instead of crying or getting mad, Paul and Silas kept 📖 working for God. ("Wow!") They sang songs and prayed to God...all night long! The other prisoners and the jail guard listened.

Let's sing a song as Paul and Silas did. Turn on the *Sing & Play Roar Music* CD, and lead children in singing "Lovely Noise." Encourage children to keep holding their friends' ankles as they sing.

SAY: Suddenly the ground began to shake. Look out! It's an earthquake!

DAY 5

HINTS FROM THE HERD

We weren't sure if preschoolers would understand how we wanted them to sit. After we demonstrated up front, they got it right away. This was a super way to explore this action-packed Bible story.

DAY 5

Help me make an earthquake. Let's stomp our feet on the ground and make a loud rumble that sounds like an earthquake. Lead children in stomping their feet and clapping their hands to create the sounds of an earthquake.

Shake your tic tac drum. **SAY:** **When the earthquake was over, the jail doors came open, and the chains fell off Paul and Silas. They were free, but they didn't run away.**

The jail guard woke up and came running over. He was sure the prisoners had gotten away and he would be in big trouble. He was so surprised to find Paul and Silas sitting there. Paul said, "Don't worry. We're all here!" The jail guard told someone to bring a light so he could count the prisoners. Let's count and see how many children are here. Lead children in counting as you tap each child on the head. **All the prisoners were there!**

The jail guard was so amazed. He realized that Paul and Silas loved Jesus and that they worked for God. The jail guard asked, "What can I do to know and love Jesus too?" Paul and Silas answered, "Believe in Jesus!"

The jail guard took Paul and Silas home with him. He took care of their hurts and gave them food. He said, "I work for God too." ("Wow!") **Then Paul and Silas told the jailer and his family about Jesus. They all believed in Jesus too.**

The next day, Paul and Silas were told that they were free. They didn't have to stay in jail. Paul and Silas kept traveling and telling more people about Jesus. That's because they worked for God.

You can work for God and tell others about Jesus too. Direct the children to gather in their Cub Crews. Distribute the "Day 5: Talk About It" questions.

DAY 5: TALK ABOUT IT

- **How did Paul and Silas show that they worked for God?** (They told people about God; they sang and praised God.)
- **How can we work for God?** (We can sing; we can share about Jesus; we can pray for others.)

Permission to photocopy these questions from Group's Serengeti Trek: Lion Cub Club Preschool Director Manual granted for local church use. Copyright © Group Publishing, Inc., P.O. Box 481, Loveland, CO 80539. www.groupvbs.com

Shake your tic tac drum, and **SAY:** **A verse from Colossians in the Bible says to work hard and cheerfully as though for the Lord. Let's sing a song to help us learn that verse.**

Have children move around and sing the following song to the tune of "The Ants Go Marching,"

I'll work hard and cheerfully
(flex muscles, then point to your smile)

For God *(point up)*,

For God! *(Point up.)*

I'll work hard and cheerfully
(flex muscles, then point to your smile)

For God *(point up)*,

For God! *(Point up.)*

In everything I say and do *(spread arms wide)*

I'll work for God *(flex muscles)*

And love God too. *(Cross arms over chest.)*

Yes, I'll work so hard and cheerfully
(flex muscles, then point to your smile)

For God *(point up)*,

For God! *(Point up.)*

DAY 5

CUB CLUB CRAFT PLAY

(up to 30 minutes)

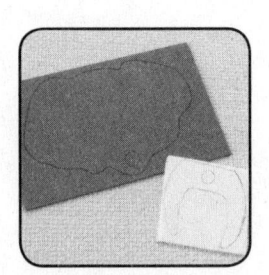

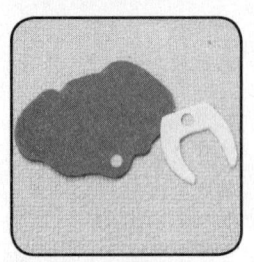

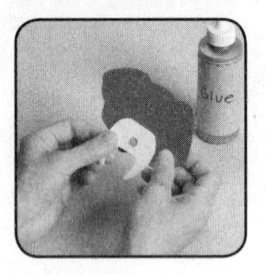

OPTION 1: LUG'S WATER BLASTERS

1. You'll work one-on-one with children for part of this craft time. Help preschoolers use the stencil and markers to trace the elephant head and tusks onto craft foam.

2. Let older preschoolers cut out the shapes while you help younger children with the cutting. (You'll need to fold the foam to cut out the circle.)

3. Place the elephant head over the tusks. Line up the holes. Let preschoolers push the trunk into the hole from the back and try to squirt each other with the water.

4. As you make the craft, talk with children about how hard elephants work. Point out that they work for people by carrying heavy loads, and they work for other elephants by making trails and digging for water. Let children share ways they can 📖 work for God.

OPTION 2: PRAISE IN PRISON

1. Give each child the Day 5 Bible Activity page from his or her Cub Club Bible Book, and write each child's name on his or her paper.

2. Direct children to glue black chenille wires over Paul and Silas to show that they're in prison. Encourage children to glue only one end of the chenille wires to the page. This way, they can bend down the wires to demonstrate how an earthquake broke down the prison doors.

3. Discuss how Paul and Silas worked for God. Talk about ways we can 📖 work for God too.

4. Turn the paper over, and discuss the Daily Challenge with the children. Be sure each child chooses and circles a challenge he or she plans to accomplish.

Permission to photocopy these options from Group's Serengeti Trek: Lion Cub Club Preschool Director Manual granted for local church use. Copyright © Group Publishing, Inc., P.O. Box 481, Loveland, CO 80539. www.groupvbs.com

OPTION 3: WORSHIP AND WORK

1. Give each child a paper plate, and allow children to use markers and stickers to decorate the back of the plates.

2. Help children lay a few foot-long crepe-paper streamers across each plate with the ends hanging off the edge. Then guide children as they put a handful of uncooked beans onto each plate.

3. Fold each plate in half, enclosing the beans and most of each streamer. Staple around the edge of the plate.

4. Let children use their shakers as they sing the following praise song to the tune of "The Mulberry Bush."

   This is the way I work for God,

   Work for God, work for God.

   This is the way I work for God

   Cheerfully each day.

5. Remind children that Paul and Silas sang and worshipped God while they were in jail.

OPTION 4: JAILED FOR GOD

1. Have a crew leader act as the jail guard. He or she should send children to "jail" with statements such as "If you're wearing sandals, you have to go to jail" or "If you have your hair in a ponytail, you have to go to jail."

2. When all the children are in jail, lead them in singing with the *Sing & Play Roar Music* CD. Then have them stomp their feet and push aside the crepe-paper streamers.

3. Lead the children in shouting, "I 📖 work for God!" Then have them give the jail guard high fives and hugs. Talk about how Paul and Silas worked for God by helping the jailer know Jesus.

Permission to photocopy these options from Group's Serengeti Trek: Lion Cub Club Preschool Director Manual granted for local church use. Copyright © Group Publishing, Inc., P.O. Box 481, Loveland, CO 80539. www.groupvbs.com

After about seventeen to twenty minutes, shake the tic tac drum, and announce that it's time for the children to clean up Cub Club Craft Play and get ready to do some other fun activities. When cleanup is complete, use your tic tac drum again, and wait for the children to gather in their Cub Crews.

DAY 5

SAY: Now we're going to watch the end of *Chadder's Serengeti Trek Adventure*. Remember, Dr. Gallstone stole the medicine, then fell into a big hole. **ASK:**

- **How do you think Chadder's adventure will end?** (Dr. Gallstone will turn in the medicine; Chadder will go home.)

SAY: Let's see if Chadder will ever get that medicine to Dr. Kim's clinic in time to help the children!

CHADDER'S ADVENTURE THEATER

(up to 15 minutes)

Lead the children to the place where you've set up a TV and a VCR or DVD player in your classroom, and let them watch the final portion of *Chadder's Serengeti Trek Adventure*.

When the video segment ends, **SAY:** Chadder sure learned a lot about God on his adventure! **ASK:**

- **What did you like best about Chadder's adventure?** (He was silly; seeing all the animals; he was smarter than Dr. Gallstone.)

- **How did Chadder and Jabari work for God at the clinic?** (They swept; they cleaned; they made the kids laugh.)

- **How can you work for God?** (Help my mom; obey my teacher.)

SAY: Chadder and Jabari helped Dr. Kim do hard jobs around the clinic. And they did the work cheerfully, just as the Bible tells us to do. They worked for God! You can work for God too! ("Wow!")

WATERING HOLE SNACKS

(up to 15 minutes)

Have the children sit at tables or in another eating area. Show children the yummy snack that looks like Paul and Silas in prison. Lead the children in a simple prayer of thanksgiving. Then give each child a napkin or paper towel, a snack, and a cup half-filled with water. Keep handy a supply of wet wipes for kids to clean their hands and paper towels to wipe up any spills. When the children have finished their snacks, have them throw away their cups and other trash. Shake the tic tac drum, and **SAY:** Let's get ready to gather the rest of the supplies for our Operation Kid-to-Kid school kits!

OPERATION KID-TO-KID™

(up to 5 minutes)

Have the Cub Crews assemble near the Operation Kid-to-Kid posters. Point to the posters and **SAY:** We've had so much fun this week learning about Jesus! These are some kids in Africa who need to learn more about Jesus too. They want to go to school and learn to read. Then they can read all these amazing stories from God's Word! We've been collecting things to help them—things like notebooks and pencils and crayons. When we send the school supplies to Africa, we'll be sharing God's love with kids like Semira, Ajani, and Muna. This is one way you and I can 📖 work for God! ("Wow!")

See if any children brought in additional school supplies today. Let children bring up their items while others cheer for them. Quickly count the number of items you've collected. **SAY:** Wow! We have [number of items] school supplies collected! What a great way to 📖 work for God. ("Wow!")

If you'll be going outdoors for Preschool Playtime, have the children hold on to their lion's tails and follow their crew leaders outside.

DAY 5

TREK TIPS

Don't make a big fuss if some children never brought in their items. Your Serengeti Trek Director may have purchased or collected extra supplies to fill the bags. If not, go ahead and put what you can in the bags, and put stickers on the bags that are incomplete.

PRESCHOOL PLAYTIME

(up to 20 minutes)

Take children outdoors, have them visit their favorite Cub Club Craft Play stations again, or let them engage in unstructured play. If you choose to go outdoors, intersperse some of the following activities with unstructured play.

DAY 5

TREK TIPS

Explain that, although only one Time for Everything *book will fit into the bag, the others will be sent to African children who don't go to school.*

OPTION 1: OPERATION KID-TO-KID™ ASSEMBLY

Have children take turns taking one object from each of the Operation Kid-to-Kid collection boxes. Let children place their items in one-gallon resealable plastic bags until each bag is complete.

As children assemble the school supply kits, have them tell you what each item is used for. Talk to the children about fun things they do with school supplies. Point out that as they work to make these special kits for other children, they're 📖 working for God.

When the bags are full, take the *Time for Everything* book from each child's Cub Club Bible Book. Let children look through the little books and talk about how the children in Africa will learn about God's love. Then put one of the books in a school supply kit. (Collect the rest and place them in a box.) Have each crew gather around its school supply kit, and tell the Cub Crew Leaders to pray, asking God to be with the children who will receive the kits.

OPTION 2: WORK LIKE AN ELEPHANT

Use the lion tails to make a large circle at one end of your playing area. Gather children, pool noodles, and a few playground balls at the other end.

Explain that elephants use their long trunks to work and help each other. Show children the pool noodles, and explain that kids will use these "trunks" to move the balls into the circle.

Let each child take a turn using a pool noodle to push a ball into the circle. Then the child should carry his or her "trunk" back to the group so the next child can try. Remind children that Paul and Silas worked for God by telling people about Jesus. Talk about ways that children can work for God.

Permission to photocopy these options from Group's Serengeti Trek: Lion Cub Club Preschool Director Manual granted for local church use. Copyright © Group Publishing, Inc., P.O. Box 481, Loveland, CO 80539. www.groupvbs.com

OPTION 3: SHAKE, SHAKE, SHAKE THE JAILHOUSE

Choose two children to be Paul and Silas. Have the rest of the children make a "prison" by standing in a circle and holding hands. Direct Paul and Silas to stand inside the circle. Remind children that in today's Bible story, God used an earthquake to shake the jail where Paul and Silas were prisoners.

Direct Paul and Silas to go around to the jail doors (where the hands are connected) and knock on them, saying, "I [picture] work for God."

Call out "Earthquake!" Then lead children in the following rhyme.

Rumble, rumble, rumble *(stomp feet),*

Shake, shake, shake *(shake hands in the air),*

Here comes a mighty, mighty earthquake.

After saying the rhyme, tell children to let go of the hands they're holding to show how the prison walls broke. Have Paul and Silas trade places with two other children, and begin the game again.

OPTION 4: FREE PLAY

If you're outdoors, let the children play with outdoor toys, such as balls, soap bubbles, or sidewalk chalk. Children would also enjoy playing on outdoor playground equipment if it's available. If you're indoors, let the children play with classroom toys, such as blocks, stuffed animals, or a water table. As the children play, look for opportunities to review today's Point and Bible story.

Permission to photocopy these options from Group's Serengeti Trek: Lion Cub Club Preschool Director Manual granted for local church use. Copyright © Group Publishing, Inc., P.O. Box 481, Loveland, CO 80539. www.groupvbs.com

After about seventeen to twenty minutes, shake the tic tac drum, and announce that it's time for the children to clean up Preschool Playtime and get ready to do some other fun activities. When cleanup is complete, use your tic tac drum again, and wait for the children to gather in their Cub Crews.

DAY 5

BIBLE MEMORY BUDDIES

(up to 10 minutes)

Hold up a Lug Bible Memory Buddy and **SAY:** **This is my friend Lug. He's an elephant, and elephants are big and strong. They work to help other elephants find food, or they make paths through the tall grass. Lug reminds me to work for God.** ("Wow!") **Let's pretend we're elephants working for God!**

Have children each hold one arm in front of them like an elephant trunk. **SAY:** **Use your long trunk to pat a friend on the head.** Pause while children follow your directions. **Now use your long trunk to give someone a hug.** Pause while children follow your directions. **See if you can use your long trunk to give a friendly wave.** Pause while children follow your directions. **Now use your trunk to give a high five to another elephant.** Pause while children follow your directions. Then have children gather with their crews.

SAY: **I want each of you working elephants to have a special gift. As your crew leaders give you a Lug Bible Memory Buddy, they'll remind you of our Bible verse, which says to work hard and cheerfully as though for the Lord. Crew leaders should say, "[Child's name] cheerfully works for God."**

Distribute Bible Memory Buddies, and have crew leaders give them out with the above affirmation. Make sure the children place Lug in their Bible Buddy Drums with the rest of their Bible Memory Buddies. Explain that children will take home their Bible Memory Buddies today!

Direct Cub Crew Leaders to collect the children's crafts and everything that has collected in their Crew Bags during the week. Have crew leaders set the things in the area where children will be picked up by their parents.

THE MANE EVENT

(up to 20 minutes)

Lead children to The Mane Event. The Mane Event Leader will greet the children and show them where to sit. Today children will present all the Operation Kid-to-Kid school supply kits and enjoy a wonderful celebration.

When the Mane Event Leader dismisses everyone, have the preschoolers remain seated with their Cub Crew Leaders until parents or caregivers arrive to pick up their children. Or take them back to Lion Cub Club, and wait for parents to pick them up there.

Remind the children to take today's Bible Activity page and other projects with them when they leave. Take a moment to have the children thank their crew leaders for being such special friends to them during VBS. Be sure to thank parents and caregivers for bringing their children to Serengeti Trek.

SAFARI SING-ALONG

Preschoolers love to sing, so here are a few songs you can intersperse with your activities. Sing these songs while kids are traveling, playing, waiting in line for the restroom, eating snacks, or when you just happen to have a few extra minutes.

These songs will remind kids to 📖 work for God.

WORK HARD

(Sing to the tune of "The Ants Go Marching.")

I'll work hard and cheerfully *(flex muscles, then point to your smile)*

For God *(point up),*

For God! *(Point up.)*

I'll work hard and cheerfully *(flex muscles, then point to your smile)*

For God *(point up),*

For God! *(Point up.)*

In everything I say and do *(spread arms wide)*

I'll work for God *(flex muscles)*

And love God too. *(Cross arms over chest.)*

Yes, I'll work so hard and cheerfully *(flex muscles, then point to your smile)*

For God *(point up),*

For God! *(Point up.)*

THIS IS THE WAY I WORK

(Sing to the tune of "The Mulberry Bush.")

This is the way I work for God,

Work for God, work for God.

This is the way I work for God

Cheerfully each day.

IN THE JAIL

(Sing to the tune of "London Bridge.")

Paul and Silas in the jail,

In the jail, in the jail.

Paul and Silas in the jail

Worked for God.

Paul and Silas sang and prayed,

Sang and prayed, sang and prayed.

Paul and Silas sang and prayed.

They worked for God!

LION CUB CLUB

LION CUB CLUB

Permission to photocopy this sign from Group's Serengeti Trek: Lion Cub Club Preschool Director Manual granted for local church use.
Copyright © Group Publishing, Inc., P.O. Box 481, Loveland, CO 80539. www.groupvbs.com

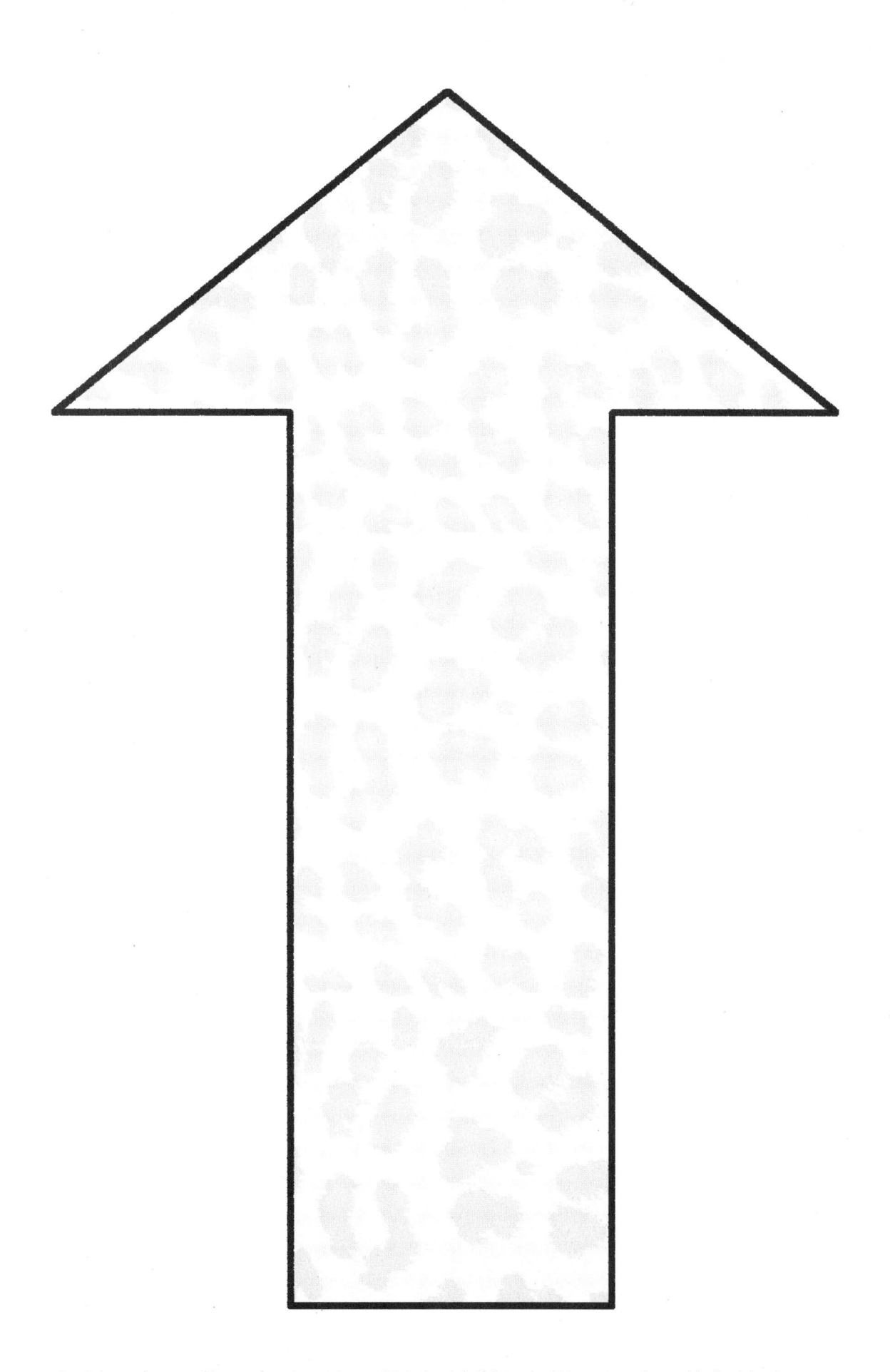

Permission to photocopy this arrow from Group's Serengeti Trek: Lion Cub Club Preschool Director Manual granted for local church use.
Copyright © Group Publishing, Inc., P.O. Box 481, Loveland, CO 80539. www.groupvbs.com

weave faith into life

FaithWeaver®
Sunday school curriculum
helps learners of all ages—
infants through adults
—weave faith into their daily lives.

Discover how it can make a difference in YOUR church.

Group's FaithWeaver
Weaving Faith Into Life

- FREE SAMPLES at www.faithweaver.com
  (in Canada www.GroupCanada.ca)
- Call toll-FREE 1-800-747-6060, ext. 1391 today
  ...or check with your favorite Christian supplier.

Bring the 1 thing to your church with **Group**

All New! for 2004

Sunday School for Toddlers–Grade 6

Grades 5 & 6
Group's Hands-On Bible Curriculum
Easy for Teachers! Fun for Kids!
Learning Lab
Teach as Jesus Taught!
New! Bible Discovery PAK

Tested Formula for LASTING BIBLE IMPACT!

Both kids and teachers love Hands-On Bible Curriculum® because:

* Life is easier for teachers! This time-tested curriculum requires little preparation each week!
* Kids have fun! It's easy to keep students' attention while they connect with Bible truths!
* Volunteers rejoice as they watch children grow! Recruiting is a pleasure when eager teachers return again and again!
* Unique Learning Labs packed with gizmos and kid-tested Bible Discovery Paks make Bible learning absolutely fun and unforgettable!

← Amazing!

Starting in fall 2004, all Learning Labs® will include NEW Bible Discovery Paks! Bursting with fun! A unique new pak every quarter in every age level uses thematic activities to reinforce Bible points.

← Available Now!

The NEW Hands-On Bible™
A kid-friendly version of God's Word crammed with new, fun, hands-on activities that correspond with Hands-On Bible Curriculum.

Hands On Bible — Experience the Fun! Live the Truth! NLT

Check Out Our Latest Developments!

oh ho! Group

Our puppets are ← ALL NEW!

Kids find these furry friends irresistible. Plus, Cuddles, Whiskers, and Pockets want to help kids learn. They're a terrific teaching tool!

Call Now for your FREE SAMPLER KIT!
1-800-747-6060 ext. 1464
or order samplers online at
www.HandsonBible.com

Bring the 1 thing™ to your church with **Group**

Growth Explodes Here!

Group's FaithWeaver Friends™ midweek!

www.fwfriends.com
FREE SAMPLE

- Preschool and elementary kids grow in their relationship with Jesus
- Multi-age small groups encourage learning and relationship-building
- Discovery Center options provide flexibility to meet your time and space needs
- Journaling helps kids apply the Bible Point to their lives
- Weekly Challenges™ put kids' faith into action
- Kid-friendly program encourages kids to reach out and invite their friends

1-800-747-6060 ext. 1457

Bring the 1 thing™ to your church with Group